Mama Needs a Time-Out:

Daily Getaways for the Mom's Soul

HEATHER RIGGLEMAN

LIVINGSTONE BOOKS
www.eCPublishingGroup.com

Endorsements

"Young moms are short on time, yet desperate for encouragement. With humor and empathy, Heather Riggleman's short 'love notes' will point them to the God who knows their name, loves them immeasurably, and longs to guide them in this crucial calling of mothering."

—**Dee Brestin,** author of *The Friendships of Women* and *Falling in Love with Jesus*

"Heather offers bite-sized pieces of scripture in thought-provoking chapters designed to encourage modern-day moms. If you want to learn and grow both personally and spiritually at the same time, read this book!"

—**Mary Byers,** author of *The Mother Load: How to Meet Your Needs While Caring for Your Family*

"As a mother of two and woman of faith, I found a strong connection with, 'I Call Him By Name.' The author's naked truth about the struggles and triumphs of motherhood are easily relatable. It's a perfect book for any mom who wants to use scripture to help bring encouragement to life's everyday challenges."

—**Leslie Means,** author of *Ella B. Bella and the Magic Pink Shoes* and the Co-Host for *Good Morning Nebraska*

"After hearing 'MOMMY' all day once, I asked my toddler to call me 'Jen' for the rest of the day. Mommy, Mama, Mom . . . we hear our name called constantly. Motherhood is so incredible and so hard. 'I Call Him By Name' not only acknowledges the challenges of parenting, but it describes the powerful names of God and reminds us that He is the strength and patience and wisdom and energy we all need to be the incredible mothers He created us to be."

—**Jen Hatmaker,** author of 9 books including *A Modern Girl's Guide to Bible Study* and *Out of the Spin Cycle: Devotions to Lighten Your Mother Load*

"Heather Riggleman is amazingly insightful in her new book, *Mama Needs a Time-Out*. Beautifully relating the various names of God with the real-life challenges busy mothers face, Heather candidly draws from her own personal 'mama' journey and helps mothers know God is real in real life. For every mother who longs to know God more, this book is definitely for you!"

—**Stephanie Shott,** is founder of The M.O.M. Initiative, author of *Understanding What Matters Most* and an international speaker

"I think this book is awesome! Truly, it is fun yet thought-provoking and insightful. Heather does a great job of using her real life examples to make it genuine and relatable. Exactly what I and other mama's out there need to hear about our God! Thanks Heather!"

—**Robbi Gould,** just another everyday mom

"As a mother who's been (and still is) in the trenches, I appreciate Heather's honesty, humor, and heart for moms. I plan to take some 'time out' with this book to be entertained, encouraged, and challenged in the journey God has called me to. Every mom should do the same."

—**Kelley Mathews,** Christian Living Editor at FaithVillage.com

"Moms long to know that God is real and present with them in the nitty-gritty, day-to-day aspects of their mothering. Through exploring the meaning of several of God's names, Heather gives moms the assurance not only that God is present in every moment of their day, but that He's there in exactly the way they need. *Mama Needs a Time-Out* will bless and encourage every mom, no matter what stage of parenting they're in."

Megan Breedlove, best-selling author of *Manna for Moms*

Mama Needs a Time-Out: Daily Getaways for the Mom's Soul

© Copyright, 2012 Heather Riggleman

Published by eChristian in association with the Books & Such Literary Agency,
  52 Mission Circle, Suite 122,
  PMB 170, Santa Rosa, CA 95409-5370,
  www.booksandsuch.com.

First printing in 2012 by eChristian, Inc.
  eChristian, Inc.
  2235 Enterprise Street, Suite 140
  Escondido, CA 92029
  http://echristian.com

ISBN: 978-1-61843-193-6

Scriptures are taken from THE HOLY BIBLE, NEW INTERNATIONAL VERSION®, NIV® Copyright © 1973, 1978, 1984, 2011 by Biblica, Inc.™ Used by permission. All rights reserved worldwide.

Scripture quotations marked NLT are taken from the Holy Bible, New Living Translation, copyright © 1996, 2004. Used by permission of Tyndale House Publishers, Inc., Wheaton, Illinois 60189. All rights reserved.

(The author has capitalized any reference to God.)

Cover and interior design by Larry Taylor

Produced with the assistance of The Livingstone Corporation. Project staff includes: Dan Balow, Afton Rorvik, Ashley Taylor, Linda Taylor, Lois Jackson and Tom Shumaker

Printed in the United States of America

19 18 17 16 15 14 13 12 8 7 6 5 4 3 2 1

Dedication

Grandma Iris Shaw,
You planted the seeds, and we are harvesting the faith.
Take care of Alex until I come home.

Deuteronomy 29:29

Table of Contents

How This Book Was Conceived 1
From Me to You 6
EL ROI: The God Who Sees Me 7
    1. I'm Invisible
    2. The Hidden Years
YAHWEH JIREH: The Lord Will Provide 15
    3. I Need a Miracle Here
    4. How Much Longer?
EL CHAY: The Living God 23
    5. You Mean There Is a God?
    6. Battling Our Insecurities
YAHWEH SHAMMAH: The Lord Is There 35
    7. He Is There
    8. The Lord Is There, Too
MACHSEH: God Is My Refuge 45
    9. A Place of Refuge from the Kids, Please!
    10. You Are My Strong Tower
ELOHIM: Creator 53
    11. You Created Me for This?
    12. When I Grow Up
EL SHADDAY: Almighty God 63
    13. Nothing Is Impossible with Him
    14. He Keeps His Promises
EL OLAM: The Everlasting God 71
    15. When Nothing Else Seems to Last
    16. He's Not Finished with You Yet
YAHWEH ROI: The Lord Is My Shepherd 79
    17. Sheep ... Really?
    18. I Can Barely Shepherd My Own Sheep!
ESH OKLAH & EL KANNA: God Is a Jealous God; God Is a Consuming Fire ... 89
    19. Striking a Balance
    20. American Idol
YAHWEH: Lord 99
    21. Yahweh Spells What?
    22. Iron Will

ADONAY: Master ... 109
    23. Who's the Boss?
    24. Masters in Disguise
YAHWEH ROPHE: The Lord Who Heals ... 119
    25. Speedy Recovery
    26. Redeemed
YAHWEH SHALOM: The Lord Is Peace ... 129
    27. Peace Within
    28. Be Still
YAHWEH NISSI: The Lord Is My Banner ... 139
    29. Raising Up Soldiers
    30. Where I Belong
ISH: Husband ... 149
    31. All the Single Ladies
    32. The Seven-Year Itch (Four Years Later)
SHOPPET: The Lord Is My Judge ... 159
    33. The Ultimate Judge
    34. Frenemies
MIQWEH YISRAEL: The Lord Is Hope ... 169
    35. Hope Is Spelled M-I-Q-W-E-H Y-I-S-R-A-E-L
    36. Here's Hoping
MELEK: King of Kings ... 179
    37. Sounds Like an Onion to Me
    38. Modern-Day Princess
YAHWEH TSURI: The Lord Is My Rock ... 189
    39. In His Hands
    40. Heart Is Where the Home Is
ABBA: Father, Daddy ... 197
    41. The Father
    42. Daddy
Group Study and Discussion Guide ... 208
A Few Thoughts ... 214
Sources ... 216

PREFACE

How This Book Was Conceived

*My life is worth **nothing** to me **unless** I use it for finishing the work assigned me by the Lord Jesus—the work of telling others the Good News about the wonderful grace of God.*

Acts 20:24 NLT (emphasis mine)

This was supposed to be a time of discovery and relaxation; instead, I was in tears as I rocked my fussy eight-month-old daughter. Here I was in the majestic mountains of Colorado for the Colorado Christian Writers Conference trying to juggle my family, attend workshops, meet with editors and authors, and learn new writing techniques. Instead of enjoying the surroundings, fellowship, and family, I was bawling my eyes out trying not to shake my daughter. For reasons I could not understand, she had been crying for nearly four hours. No amount of nursing, walking, shushing, pleading, begging, praying, or screaming helped. Tori continued to cry.

For months I looked forward to coming here; it was part of a new chapter in my life. All my chica-mamas from my Bible study group sent me here through gifts of money because they believed in me. They knew without a doubt I had a story to tell or rather that I had a gift. I wasn't so sure, but I did know that this new role beyond mothering literally fired up the depths of my heart.

After the third hour of Tori's screaming, I lay beside her and began crying myself. I asked God, "Why is this happening? This is supposed to be a time of relaxation and refreshment so I can learn if writing is what You are calling me to do." Truthfully, I admit I yelled at Him that I surrendered. I told Him He could have it His way even though I didn't understand why Tori had chosen this day and this place to scream nonstop.

Then I heard it, *Surrender.*

PREFACE

"Um God, I don't know if You noticed, but I'm pretty sure I made that clear. I mean I'm pretty sure that anyone in the hall could have heard me scream 'I surrender.'" Surely the face down prone position I had taken while calling His name showed obvious signs of surrender.

Surrender it all.

"What? What's that supposed to mean. Is this a joke? Now is SO not the time for a deep spiritual moment or conversation, pal!" (Note: This baby Christian is still in the process of learning to be reverent and not sarcastic with God. I have made great progress... seriously.)

You've surrendered your heart, your talents, and your life. You've not surrendered control of your family. Let go and just be. Am I not the God who provides? Am I not the God of comfort? Am I not the God of healing? All these things I am prepared to give you when you stop fighting Me.

"Fighting? How am I fighting?"

Let go and let it be.

It wasn't until nearly 45 minutes later that Tori stopped her screaming episode. Everyone thinks it was a "God thing," however, I believe it was because Tylenol and milk finally took effect. What baby can resist mama's milk laced with Tylenol?

The rest of the trip I was frazzled and perplexed by this conversation and disappointed by the experience of it all after we returned home. It also didn't help that Tori ran a high fever for twelve days afterward.

A few weeks later as I was still pouting and wondering what I was supposed to have gotten out of the conference, I was alone downstairs reading my daily devotional when God spoke to me again. I began noticing the different names He was called. He is our Healer, Redeemer, Avenger, Provider, Alpha, Omega, Judge, Savior, and the list goes on. I became intrigued with the history and origin of the names and began tracing them back to their Greek and Hebrew roots. It tied in nicely with the conversations my women's Bible study group had over the names of God the year before. I still had the printed page of God's names tucked away in my journal.

As a recent convert to being a passionate Christian, I was puzzled by the different names God was given throughout the Bible. Though I was learning

PREFACE

about God and His Son through reading my Bible, devotions, and church, I still felt like I didn't really understand *who* He was. Here is this God who is the master of the universe, who can snuff out my life in an instant, who can and did choose to call me and redeem my pitiful life, who knew everything about me and yet, I only had head knowledge of who He is. I wanted to really *know* Him. After all, if I was going to be willing to sacrifice my life in an instant and become a slave for Christ, I thought it might be a good idea to know the depths of His heart.

His voice came loud and clear as did His instructions.

You have not been given a spirit of fear, but one of love. Write a devotional; use My names.

By the way, if you ever think God has given you a task or dream so monumentally big that you know you could never complete it on your own, think again. If this big dream leaves you quaking in your sweatpants or causes you to question your sanity, it's probably God. If you begin to question there is truth in the theory that women's brains do shrink after pregnancy or you're wondering if you have hit menopause early, then I can pretty much guarantee it is God speaking to you. No dream or task (including motherhood) can ever be completed unless God's hand is on it. So, as I sat there pondering His instructions, I began asking mere human beings for their advice about what I heard.

Me: So do you think I have a gift? Do you think I should try to write this devotion about God's names? We've only been Bible thumpers for like five years.

Husband: Sure, why not? What else are you going to do to keep sane around here? You can put words together that make sense, so do it. (Note: My husband comes from Wyoming and reads one book per decade.)

Me: So is this crazy? Can I write a book someone would want to read?

Audra (a.k.a. close friend, knows me so well she isn't fazed over my weekly emotional tirades)**:** If God is calling you to it, He can bring you through it. After all, you won't be writing it, He will be.

Me: Well thanks for the vote of confidence, smarty pants.

Me: I think I'll take a stab at it.

PREFACE

Angela (my best friend who brought me to Jesus. In the beginning of my journey as a Christian we had "I'm mad at you" sessions which would then involve our husbands as we would leave messages on each other's answering machines. Our husbands would then relay the message and call the other husband back)**:** So you're thinking about writing a novel huh?

Me: Novel? What's a novel?

Angela: It's a book with pages and a story in it. Are you gonna write about your family? You could probably make millions and have sequels with all the drama. It's better than watching a soap!

Me: I'm going to take that as a compliment. So, do you think I can write?

Angela: Heather, you have a gift.

Nancy (fellow church member and Facebook stalker)**:** So I hear you're thinking about writing a book? If it's anything like your Facebook posts, I can tell ya half of us gals can't wait to get our hands on it.

Wendy, Shelley, Marla, Janet (a few other fellow Facebook stalkers)**:** You need to write more stories about Elijah. I hop on the net every morning wondering what the boy is going to do to send you into a straitjacket. Looking forward to reading it.

No pressure here. Apparently my son is a wealth of material for writing. (More later about that spirited, strong-willed child who will send me to an early grave. Ok one note—I'm honestly surprised he made it to his fifth birthday.)

Anyway, moving on, I took on this endeavor because I wanted to know the essence of God and why He has so many names. I wanted to know the depth of His Spirit and why He loved me so much. My past is full of more than a few bad choices. It's filled with decay and regret. How could the God of the universe want to have fellowship with me? More importantly, why would He want to use my voice, or my journey into motherhood for that matter, to reach out to other moms? I hardly have it together. I'm not a role model unless you're into the Army boot camp style as a mothering method. Furthermore I'd rather not humiliate myself in setting up a dream so big for everyone to see (stupid Facebook), only to fail.

Over these last couple of years of writing and parenting, I'm amazed at just how perfectly each of God's names fits into mothering. Whether it's a story

PREFACE

in the Bible about seeking Him as a Refuge or looking to Him as a Husband, every name sheds light on the depths of who He is. It brings a new dimension to my love for Him. It deepens the passion I have for His Word and His Son.

It's my hope that my stories and my words will shed new meaning on His names for you and that you will fall more in love with Him. If not, at the very least I hope you get a few good laughs from some of my mothering mayhems and know you're not alone in that journey either!

From Me to You

Have you ever really wondered who God is? God is the One who created the world around us that displays His glory. From the air we breathe, to setting boundaries on time, He created it all. God then wrote a book called the Bible in which He is the main character. He wrote the Bible so that we might get a glimpse of His character and His glory. He wrote it so that we might fall in love with Him. He wrote it so that we could find Him in the day-to-day things.

As I studied the Bible, I became intrigued by all the different characteristics and names that God was called. I wanted to know Him better and so did my Sonrise Women's Bible study group. This book was birthed to help moms like me catch a more intimate glimpse of God on a daily basis. Through identifying God's different names you will be drawn into a deeper relationship with Him and will pray more effectively.

This book highlights twenty-two different names of God, each relating to the motherhood challenges we face on a day-to-day basis. You'll find practical help to become more aware of His presence in *Mama Needs a Time-Out*. Each chapter includes what I call a "Love Note" from God. My husband used to leave hot pink sticky notes around the house to remind me of his love for me. Much in the same way our God loves us and has left us little love notes through the entire Bible. One of God's passions is to show us how much He loves us. The Bible is honestly one giant hot pink sticky note. Each "Love Note" nugget of Scripture is for you to take to heart and treasure as you "Call Him by Name" in a closing prayer.

Now . . . let me share with you the first time I became aware of God in the middle of motherhood and feeling invisible.

EL ROI

The God Who Sees Me

Genesis 16:11-14; Psalm 139:1-12

*She gave this name to the L*ORD *who spoke to her:
"You are the God who sees me," for she said,
"I have now seen the One who sees me."*

GENESIS 16:13

I'm Invisible

"Elijah, Cheyenne, pick up your toys. It's time to come in!" I hollered from the stoop of our front porch while balancing Tori on my hip as she clapped her hands and drooled. The children paused for a second as if they weren't quite sure they heard something and then continued playing.

Exasperated, I yelled a little louder. "Hey! It's time to come in. Pick up your toys!" They still ignored me. I threw my husband an irritated look as he came around the corner from the garage. He called to our oldest two. They looked back from where they were playing and came running to Daddy with their toys in tow. *Great,* I thought to myself. *Just great! They seem to only have ears for Dad, and I'm the one who carried them in my body for nine months!*

It hit me full force that evening—I'm invisible! Where did I go? How did the role of mothering take over my whole identity? Furthermore, why in the world didn't my family see it or appreciate me? They didn't thank me for the clean floors or the socks paired and put away in drawers. They didn't notice that I had slaved in the kitchen all afternoon to come up with something tasty for dinner that everyone liked. Just for the record, in my house coming up with a universal meal is a major triumph considering that Elijah hates vegetables, Cheyenne hates meat, and my husband doesn't think it's a meal unless steak and potatoes are involved.

After getting the kids into bed, I wearily began straightening the living room. It was more of a safety precaution so I wouldn't step on a toy, lose my balance, and break my neck in the middle of the night. "Not that anyone would notice," I grumbled. That's when a frumpy figure caught my eye. I couldn't believe the woman I saw in the mirror. She was a faded version of the vibrant Heather that I remembered. I wanted to cry. I hated this curvier body that I acquired after the birth of my third child. Neither did I appreciate the short, "budget friendly, too busy to fix it" haircut I also acquired during my pregnancy. I hardly had the extra cash for indulging in good makeup other than what I could find for under $8.00 at Walmart, and I hadn't bought new clothes in over a year. I couldn't even remember the last time I visited the salon for highlights! Wanting to be a good mother, I had put my children and their needs first. Little by little I had let myself fall apart.

I used to observe sleep deprived women in stores wearing shabby, worn-out T-shirts and no makeup. They pushed their carts down the aisle while attempting to keep their children from throwing another tantrum. "I'll never let myself look like that," I used to think to myself. "I'll be the best Mama Diva this town has ever seen. It's a piece of cake!" (Yes, I thought of myself as a diva, and if you met my family, you'd understand. Oh, and yes, I tend to be a bit fashion oriented.) But that was before I became pregnant with my second and then third child after an unintended eight-year gap between my first two children. God had shown me much mercy with my oldest child. Cheyenne was and still is a very sweet child. I wasn't prepared for the challenges of mothering two more children who were anything but "easy."

Looking in the mirror, I regretted giving my whole body over to the process, not to mention all those extra tacos I ate. While pinching the lovely donut layer around my waist, I wondered how I had managed to become a faded, invisible version of myself. Not only had my needs become invisible, my job of running the home and nurturing my children had become invisible to my family.

Still sullen and miserable from what I saw in the mirror, I opened my prayer journal trying to push my "poor me" thoughts away. God then gently reminded me of who He is and that I was not invisible to Him.

My eyes came to rest on notes about the woman, Hagar. In Genesis 16:1-14, Sarai, who had tried for years to give her husband a child, finally gave Abram her servant, Hagar, so she could bear his children. (It was not uncommon in those days for an infertile woman to start a family using her servants.) Hagar had no choice but to obey her mistress. When she became pregnant, she began to treat Sarai with contempt. Sarai complained to her husband who told her she could do as she wished with Hagar. Therefore, in a scorned woman mode she began treating Hagar harshly, and Hagar ran away. An angel of the Lord appeared to Hagar in the desert telling her that God had heard her desperate cries. Even though Hagar was alone in the wilderness sitting next to a well, God was aware of her hurts, her thoughts, and her needs. Hagar then addressed God as El Roi, "the God who sees me."

God gently reminded me He knows the number of hairs on my head. He knows my thoughts and when I wake up and lie down. I am not invisible to Him. As a matter of fact, He cares about everything I do and promises to walk beside me as I press on to take care of my family.

There are many moments in motherhood when we feel alone, desolate, and locked within the four walls we call home. Mothering is hard work. I can't think of any other career that has an expectancy of at least eighteen years and being on the job twenty-four hours a day, seven days a week. The end achievement is to survive our children's antics and launch them into the world to be successful and to love God.

It's amazing to think the God of the universe cares about me folding socks. He cares that I change diapers, and He cares that I feel alone. He cares that I feel frumpy and invisible. And He cared enough to space my childbearing eight years apart so I wouldn't be a complete train wreck.

El Roi watches over all I do. He watches over you, too. He loves you and wants to tell you so.

Mama's Time-Out

- Does it give you great comfort to know that God sees you exactly where you are?
- Take a moment to thank God for His ever-watchful eye and pray that He increases your awareness of His presence. You'll be glad you did!

Today's Love Note

You have searched me, LORD,
and you know me.
You know when I sit and when I rise;
you perceive my thoughts from afar.
You discern my going out and my lying down;
you are familiar with all my ways.

Psalm 139:1-3

I Call Him By Name

El Roi, these thoughts are too much for me to comprehend. I cannot imagine that the God of the universe knows everything about me. I cannot fathom that You see me. You know when I'm weary; You know when I feel invisible. Help me to remember that I'm not invisible to You. Let Your presence shine as I fold socks, wash dishes, and rock my little ones to sleep. Thank You for loving me in a way that I cannot imagine. Amen.

The Hidden Years

Ever feel like you landed on a new planet when you became a mom? There was a whole new being in your life, not to mention new words, new routines, new waking hours, new wardrobe, and a new body. Whether or not you like all aspects, it's up to you. I, however, mainly despised the body part! I also didn't like how enclosed I felt within the four walls of my home. Days ran together and turned into weeks. Before I knew it, it had been a whole month since I embarked on a journey outside my home. I hadn't even seen friends much less the inside of my car. I was so caught up in caring for my newborn son who had a severe case of jaundice, I did not realize the amount of time that passed. When I did, I was in for a shock. Apparently there is no "I" in Mommy. I had somehow been deposited to a different planet after I gave birth. My world didn't orbit around me anymore.

When I did venture out, I found that new language was pretty handy as I began relating to moms a whole new way. Our children were our common bond. While I was thankful other women had landed on planet Mom, I longed for and even missed the recognition I received for all my achievements in the workplace. I tucked these annoying thoughts to the back of my mind as I tried to focus on my new tasks as a mother.

Over the years as my children grew, I felt as if I were meant to do something more, to be something greater. Granted I did love the Queen of Casseroles and

Mommy titles my children bestowed on me, but I felt there was something greater out there I could be doing. Somehow I was waiting for this transition period to be over. If only the kids could feed and water themselves, the real adventure would begin. I would once again be recognized for my leadership abilities and administrative skills. There were days when I saw other moms running to work in crisp suits. Tucked into their SUVs I was certain they had a more noteworthy purpose than wiping runny noses. I felt invisible—maybe even hidden on this new planet of Motherhood.

"Tell me, oh mighty El Roi, what is it that You see? What is it that You have planned for me?" Surely it's more than remaining hidden at home with no one ever knowing how skilled I am in taming chaos, encouraging others to follow their dreams, or the fact that I can alphabetize my entire pantry in a matter of two hours. I was restless and wondered if I was wasting time. Maybe there was something more I should be doing other than feeding, burping, wiping, cooking, and cleaning. Do you ever feel this way—like your mothering isn't a worthy role or that you, too, are wasting time?

Let's get one thing straight: our Father God does not waste time. Take Sarah, for example. She was her grandmother's age when she birthed her son, Isaac. The years of childbearing were purposely passed up so God could reveal that He alone controls destiny and His "timing" is perfect. Hagar's time in the desert crying out to the unseen God was not wasted either. El Roi met her there. He wanted her to understand that her life as a servant was not insignificant. And though her servitude under her master had its frictional moments, God saw it all. He was with her and came to her in her time of need.

These moments of child rearing are not wasted. It's in these quiet, unseen moments that God meets us where we are. He unveils His character to us when we feel the most weak and humble. These moments are meant to refine us, perfect us, rest us, restore us, and strengthen us. I can't imagine a more crucial season in life when God is needed more than when we first land on planet Mom. We will have years in which we feel hidden at home, but not one minute is wasted. God uses these minutes and days to mold, shape, and refine us if we give ourselves over to the process.

Another noteworthy person whose life was hidden was Jesus. Practically the first three decades about Him are unknown except for snippets here and there. He wasn't known for anything other than the last three astonishing years of His life when He gave it all up as a ransom for us. God watched over Jesus since the day of His conception. God whispered, encouraged, and walked with His Son, Jesus, during the hidden years. Only in the last three years of Jesus' life do we see how God shaped His character and how God strengthened Him before He began His mission to share the love of the Father.

While we cannot compare our calling to Christ, we do know that God values each mother. Motherhood is another form of ministry, and its mission field is our children. The years we spend at home are most important. It's in the trenches of motherhood where we are used to shape our children's hearts and character to the likeness of Christ.

So whether you are new to planet Mom or have been a citizen for many years, just know that El Roi is there in the quiet moments, He is there in the chaotic moments, and He is there in the moments when you feel hidden. God sees you and He loves how you are caring for His children. If you're feeling a little too hidden and too alone, I would encourage you to go to Him and tell Him how you feel. Trust me. He's big enough to hear your thoughts and what's resting in your heart. He is ready and waiting.

Mama's Time-Out

- Does it amaze you to know that Jesus spent thirty years in seclusion before His big debut?
- During this season of motherhood, has there been a moment or season in which you felt hidden? Was there any growth in any area of your life?
- Take time to acknowledge a fellow Mommy friend for some of her talents that others may not get to see.

Today's Love Note

Being confident of this, that he who began a good work in you will carry it on to completion until the day of Christ Jesus.

Philippians 1:6

I Call Him By Name

El Roi, I thank You for every woman You have called to Your mission field. Help them to gain strength and remain confident in You and Your promises. Lord, I ask You to touch my heart today and make Your presence known to me. Give me peace and joy as I teach my kids to know and love You. Thank You, Father God, that You see me for who I really am and that You hold me in Your mighty hands. Amen.

YAHWEH JIREH

The Lord Will Provide

Genesis 22:13-14; Deuteronomy 15:4-5; Luke 12:28-34; 1 Corinthians 10:12-13;
Philippians 4:11-13, 19; 1 Timothy 6:17-19

"Father?"

"Yes, my son?" Abraham replied.

*"The fire and wood are here," Isaac said, "but where is the lamb
for the burnt offering?"*

*Abraham answered, "God himself will provide the lamb
for the burnt offering, my son."*

And the two of them went on together. . . .

Abraham looked up and there in a thicket he saw a ram caught by its horns.

*He went over and took the ram and sacrificed it as
a burnt offering instead of his son.*

So Abraham called that place The Lord Will Provide.

And to this day it is said, "On the mountain of the Lord

it will be provided."

Genesis 22:7-8, 13-14

I Need a Miracle Here

I peeked out the window as I watched the mail carrier make his rounds on our block. Not wanting him to see me in my tank top and sweatpants while waiting on the mail, I dropped the curtain back and waited five more minutes for him to deposit the mail into my box. Mail was another highlight of my day because it meant outside communication. Who knows, maybe Ed McMahon was sending me a letter to tell me how much money I'd won.

I slowly sank to my knees as I opened up another letter from our insurance company. Since the beginning of January 2010, I had seen one specialist after another because my heart would unexpectedly race while my blood pressure dropped. Then I would black out. For the last month I had needed to wear a heart monitor continuously.

The envelope was thin with a single piece of paper inside. I knew that the news the letter held would not be good. I was right! The letter stated that the procedures I had done for my heart were deemed "experimental" and they would be billing me for the entire amount of $4,500.

Oh yeah, just what I wanted to do. Squeeze more money out of our less than ideal budget for a huge bill. I sighed to myself as I looked around our tiny home as the kids romped through the living room pretending to be cars. How am I gonna take care of this?

Oftentimes we find ourselves in less than ideal circumstances wondering how our needs are going to be met. We live in a blessed country full of abundance at every turn, not to mention the independent streak inborn in every American that causes us to feel the need to stand on our own two feet and to forget that God was the one who gave us those two feet! If we are to rely on this mighty God, then where is the extra cash for the overdue electric bill? How are we going to get the brakes fixed? What about a compassionate friend to talk to in a time of crisis?

While we may never understand God's ways or ever fully know Him, He knows each of us intimately. This means He knows what our needs are better than we do. Take, for example, when Abraham first called God Yahweh Jireh. As a test of his respect and reverence for God, Abraham was told to go and sacrifice his long-awaited and precious son, Isaac. Abraham obeyed and faithfully set out on this endeavor. In the midst of what would have been Isaac's last moments, God provided a ram for the sacrifice.

How does this apply to you or me? I'm going to be transparent and tell you the amount of money currently sitting in my checking account is $423.37 to be exact. "What are your monthly bills?" you might ask. More than what I can pay. "Well, why not go to work?" you wonder. "Why are you sitting in front of your computer instead of trying to make ends meet?" Because this is where God called me. He's called me to be at home with my children.

I am educated with bachelor's degree in Criminal Justice. I could be out behind the wheel of a squad car, or monitoring parolees, or even a legal assistant in a law office; but that's not where He wants me to be at the moment. (Besides, when I applied for a position on the police department, it didn't go so well due to the fact I'm a mom. Protective moms view all citizens as potential bad guys.) I could be earning a salary of $40,000 or more a year and be living comfortably instead of stretching every penny.

I can tell you that after I felt God whispering to me to be a stay-at-home mom, we fought criticism from family members and friends. My husband and I looked at each other one evening and thought how crazy it was that we were doing this. However, we remained faithful to His call. There have been moments over the last three years in which we truly wondered if we were going to have the funds to replace the brakes, fix our furnace, pay for Tori's broken leg, send Cheyenne to camp, and so much more. When looking at our accounts and bills from a paper perspective, it doesn't add up. However, when looking at it through spiritual eyes, we see where and how He's provided. The week our van broke down and we needed $600 for the repairs, we received a refund in the mail from Chris's cafeteria plan. You guessed it! The check was for $600.

As the afternoon wore on filled with the daily domestic chores of laundry, picking up toys, and running errands, I sent up a silent prayer to God. "Okay God, I give up. It's in Your hands. If You want me at home with my kids, then You need to provide for this need. Help me to trust that You have a plan for this bill."

Later, my husband arrived home from work and handed me his cell phone. There was a message from the clinic concerning our bill. Because of the cost of the heart monitor that my doctor felt was necessary, the clinic had a meeting with the hospital they partner with. In light of our financial circumstances and the unique needs of my case, the hospital and clinic decided that they would pay the bill in full. (Tax break for corporate America works in my favor, YES!) I was shocked and amazed. God had indeed foreseen the situation and provided in a way I never expected.

The one thing I can attest to is that when it comes to providing, God is never late. His timing is always perfect. I'd love it though if He could arrive a few days sooner!

Getting back to the character of His name, God does provide. Perhaps this is how most people are introduced to Him—especially moms. We wonder how we are going to provide everything for that tiny bundle of joy. The Hebrew word *raah* means "to see" and is translated as *provide* in Genesis 22:14. "On the mountain of the LORD it will be provided." So when we are praying to Yahweh Jireh, we are praying to the God who already knows what we need. He foresaw the situation before we did and already had a plan. While we may not be a big fan of His timing or don't like how He provides for a particular situation, it gives great comfort and security to know that the God of yesterday and the God of the future is also the God who is present in our situation now. He is ever with us and knows our needs before we do.

Mama's Time-Out

 Take a jar, clean out its old contents, and decorate it. Each time God provides something for you or your family, write it on a sheet of paper and date it. You can also add answered prayers. When you or your family become discouraged or forget how He has provided, you have the moments written on paper to remind you all.

Today's Love Note

"Therefore I tell you, do not worry about your life, what you will eat or drink; or about your body, what you will wear. Is not life more than food, and the body more than clothes? Look at the birds of the air; they do not sow or reap or store away in barns, and yet your heavenly Father feeds them. Are you not much more valuable than they?"

Matthew 6:25-26

I Call Him By Name

Yahweh Jireh, it gives me great comfort and security to know that my life rests completely in Your capable hands. The hands that created the earth are also the hands that provide for my every need. You have set my days before me and have prepared to care for me just as I prepare to care for my children. I thank You that I can call You my Yahweh Jireh. In Your name I pray. Amen.

How Much Longer?

Wearily I glanced at the clock thinking it had to be getting close to nap time. It wasn't even ten o'clock yet! I still had three hours until nap time. *Somebody just please shoot me!* I thought to myself as I kicked the laundry halfheartedly down the stairs.

Suddenly it seemed as if my eardrums were breaking as Tori's screams pierced the air. Elijah had just hit her with another block for no apparent reason. Maybe it was because they have to share the same air.

"Elijah Michael, why did you hit your sister?"

No response.

"Answer me!"

"Because I say so," he replied as he glared at me.

I sighed as we headed back upstairs to another time-out. This was round four of defiance and the morning was only half over.

"How much longer, God? How much longer until I'm able to rest? Can't You just command them to fall asleep where they are standing or something?" I prayed silently as I listened to my son's shrieks of protest and Tori's cries of hurt and wanting Mommy. I was pretty sure that any second I was going to spontaneously combust from frustration and lack of sleep.

Right then the doorbell rang. It was Amber with an ice cold can of Coke, toting her little ones who distracted my children into a truce as they ran out to the backyard to play. In the trenches of everyday mothering, God not only provided an energy renewal, He provided a friendly face to help me combat cranky children.

There are more days than I care to count when I've had less than four hours of sleep, the house is a mess, and the kids have been up since 6:00 a.m. and seem to have woken up on the wrong side of the bed. What I need is a maid, a massage therapist, and a nanny! Knowing that I will never have them, I rely on the inner strength God provides each day.

God knows how much children drain us and how much it takes to nurture each one of them. Thankfully, without ever knowing it, I spent my childhood in boot camp as I helped raise my five younger siblings. Being a wife and mommy never crossed my mind. I was busy imagining being a college professor or counselor. As I became a mother of three, I knew that God had provided seventeen years of training through feeding, clothing, entertaining, and loving my siblings while my mother was going to school and working. Those experiences were especially valuable due to the age gap between my first and second born as well as the fact that my youngest two are strong willed and my oldest has inattentive attention deficit disorder combined with Asperger's.

Take a moment to examine your life. How has God provided in the department of friends? What about strength, patience, rest, and laughter? It's in these small everyday moments God is winking at us as if to say, "Hey, little mama, I know you're tired today, but I got that covered. Look to Me and you will surely find what you're looking for. Remember, I know your needs." God is there to cheer us on. He will provide what we need when we need it the most.

Mama's Time-Out

Pack up your kids and drop in on a friend who you know is having a few rough days in motherhood. With any luck your kids will distract each other while you share your favorite beverage and swap stories.

Today's Love Note

Cast your cares on the LORD
and he will sustain you;
he will never let the righteous be shaken.

Psalm 55:22

I Call Him By Name

Yahweh Jireh, I'm so thankful that before I woke up this morning You were already thinking about me. You know my needs and I'm amazed how You provide. When I'm tired, You give me rest. When I'm weak, You become my strength. When I feel that I'm falling, You give me a place to stand. Thank You for meeting my needs today, and help me to look to You as my God, the Lord who provides. Amen.

EL CHAY

The Living God

DEUTERONOMY 5:26; JOSHUA 3:9-10; 2 KINGS 19:15-16; PSALM 42:2; JEREMIAH 10:3-5

You Are Who You Are for a Reason

You are who you are for a reason.
You're part of an intricate plan.
You're a precious and perfect unique design,
Called "God's special woman or man."
You look like you look for a reason.
Our God made no mistake.
He knit you together within the womb,
You're just what He wanted to make!
The parents you had were the ones He chose,
And no matter how you may feel,
They were custom-designed with God's plan in mind,
And they bear the Master's seal.
No, that trauma you faced was not easy;
And God wept that it hurt you so.
But it was allowed to shape your heart
So that into His likeness you'd grow.
You are who you are for a reason.
You've been formed by the Master's rod.
You are who you are, Beloved,
Because there is a GOD!

© Russell Kelfer

You Mean There Is a God?

If these old walls could talk, I thought to myself as I carefully picked my way across the shattered glass and broken floorboards in my childhood home. These walls saw each tear, heard every whisper, and witnessed the breaking of our hearts. My grandmother's house had been the center of my life. It was built on land the Pima County Mine owned next to a pecan field in Suhaurita, Arizona. The walls were white; the house was stucco with adobe red trim and red sidewalks. When I was a child, the house felt so big to me. Oddly enough, eleven years later I felt like a giant coming back to the once pristine house that was now in shambles and condemned. Squatters had obviously been there leaving their mark of tattered blankets, beer cans, and needles.

Back then I didn't believe God existed. I thought religion was something to distract us from the reality of life. I grew up in a home full of domestic violence with an alcoholic, drug-addicted father and a mother who loved him too much, enabling him to continue with his addictions. By the time I was twelve, a family member took my innocence. I often wondered, if God existed, why He would have allowed all the hurt and pain in just my childhood alone. When I entered college, my thoughts were reinforced after an assault by a co-worker.

It wasn't until I was in my mid-twenties that I came to know the living God personally. After a series of well-timed events that would make anyone want to jump off a bridge, I came face-to-face with God. The night I attempted to take my life, El Chay met me in the bed I was strapped to in the Emergency Room. My blood alcohol content was .181 and rising, while the effects of the drug cocktail of prescriptions I had taken was reacting dangerously with the alcohol. Doctors and nurses scrambled to pump my stomach while several police officers held me down on the bed as I struggled not to black out. Everyone in the room was in a frenzy to save my life as a wave of peace that I had never experienced before settled over me. It was then that El Chay spoke to me.

Heather, I have great plans for you. Your time here is not over.

That moment was so powerful and so vivid that I knew with all my being that it was not a hallucination. God was real, and He was speaking to me! I stopped fighting all the doctors, nurses, and officers and surrendered to El Chay.

Within a few weeks after my near-death experience, I was over twenty thousand feet in the air on an eighteen-hour flight to China for a class assignment. Thumbing through a book my counselor had given me, I came across the words by Russell Kelfer. As I read them, God's voice intertwined with the words. God was telling me that it broke His heart when I was abused. It broke His heart even more when I couldn't understand that the ways of this world were not His ways. And yet, every day of my life He was with me. There will be a day when God will avenge what happened to me. There will be a day when we all will have to answer for what we have done in our lives.

This revelation brought healing to my wounded heart. The living God was and is heartbroken and angry for all the wrong committed against His children. However, even with all the wrong, He can create beauty out of the ashes—beauty that testifies to life and His glory.

The words of that poem whispered promises that when a heart accepts Him, the Holy Spirit begins renewing and restoring the soul into what God intends. The hurt and pain then glorify God just as the scars upon the body of Jesus glorified our Father, the living God.

Over the next few years, as I recovered from the trauma I had faced, God was in the process of breathing new life into me. The Bible became my daily bread that I craved more than food itself. It not only sustained me, it satisfied my hunger while filling the emptiness of my heart. Gone were the feelings of isolation and worthlessness and the frustration of trying to fill my life with earthly things. No amount of worldly things ever touched that part of my soul where I ached for something more. And yet within moments of surrendering my life to God, He more than filled the ache within me.

There is much to be thankful for. Each day God reminds me that I am redeemed. Each new day is a gift in itself as I roll out of bed and thank God for it and submit my day to His will. Before my toes ever touch the hardwood floors, I know that He is with me. He is watching all that I do. He is ever so real.

Meeting God in the midst of troubling circumstances sweeps us into His arms and teaches us that while we can see and touch the world around us, it will eventually fall away as God and Jesus reign. We are here on earth for a short time, only to prepare ourselves for what the living God has intended for us in the future when His Son comes for His church, His people.

Have you ever heard stories like mine? Stories where God meets someone when they've hit rock bottom? Our communities are full of them and so is the Bible. One of my favorite stories where El Chay is referenced is in the New Testament. It's the story of the woman at the well.

God's Word and His power were embodied in His Son, Jesus, who came to earth to give us living water. When Jesus walked the earth, He did something unthinkable. He spoke with a Samaritan woman.

So many things about that woman mirrored my soul. She was dirty, used, broken, and lonely. Her background made her an outcast because she had five husbands and the one she was living with at that present moment was not her husband. Her shame and pain were so great, she avoided going to the well in the cool hours of the morning so as not to face the scorn of the other women in her village who were drawing water needed for their daily duties.

Jesus met her at the well and defied the laws of their culture by speaking to her. He told her what He knew about the things of her life. And He told her about the living water He offers because He is the living God manifested in flesh.

This story embodies what God is trying to do today in our lives. Because I've accepted His living water, it tends to leak out of me and drip on others I come in contact with. There are many women in our communities who are lost and broken much like this Samaritan woman. It is up to us to be an example and a light among these women so that God can live through us to offer them the gift we have received. The light and living water will not only be passed on to these women but to their husbands and children as God fills their empty hearts.

El Chay, the living God, captures His role as Creator, Living Water, and the only living God. The gift of His living water is never in short supply for those who believe in Him. That first sip of what He has to offer will indeed change your heart and your life.

Today you may be tangled up in the hurts and fears of the past. I encourage you to get on your knees and cry out to the living God. He is alive and well, working out the plan He has for your life. Pray to Him and ask Him to meet you where you are. Ask for that refreshing sip of water He has to offer.

Mama's Time-Out

Do you know the living God? If not, are you ready to? I urge you at this very moment to ask Him into your heart in your own words or use the following prayer.

> "Heavenly Father, forgive me for living life the way I have. I don't want to live this way anymore. I don't want to feel dirty, worthless, and lonely. I acknowledge that Jesus died on the cross for my sins and that You raised Him from the dead. Dear Jesus, please forgive me and cleanse me from every sin that's grieved Your heart. Come into my heart as my personal Savior and Lord. Fill my heart with Your living water today as I surrender full control of my life to You. I pray this in Jesus' name. Amen."

Today's Love Note

"But whoever drinks the water I give [her] will never thirst. Indeed, the water I give [her] will become in [her] a spring of water welling up to eternal life."

John 4:14

I Call Him By Name

El Chay, what a strange and wondrous name. It means You exist. It means You are the living, breathing God whom I can talk to and count on in all of life's circumstances. I thank You and praise You for healing my heart. I thank You for creating me just the way I am. I thank You that You are the God of my life. Thank You for the refreshing living water that is a spring in my heart. I know that I'm so blessed to be called Your beloved. Thank You, Lord, for the life You've given me. In Your name I pray. Amen.

Battling Our Insecurities

At a resort in Cancun I tried to wear a bikini, but it turned into a disaster. Come on girls, I bet you can already guess why. One word—insecurity! It didn't help that as I laid on the beach with my husband, a woman near us decided to tan topless. One glance quickly helped size up my situation. Implants and all, the woman had everything I didn't. I tucked my feelings away and instead focused on how rude she was not to be considerate of the values and beliefs of others.

Upon returning home, my feelings of inadequacy took root and quickly grew out of control. I constantly compared myself to other women who were more put together than I was in my non-designer outfits, not to mention I didn't have the extra cash for manicures, highlights, tanning, or cute bags and shoes. Others made me feel insecure because they were a better parent than me. They would talk kindly to their child using Love and Logic® while I used the Mobster Method—better known as finding what my children liked and threatening to take it out! And others were always doing something with friends, while I felt forgotten and left out.

I was miserable because of my constant comparisons, but the more I resolved to work on myself in the departments of looks, materialistic things, and popularity, the farther I sank into a hole of despair. It wasn't until I attended Beth Moore's conference, "So Long, Insecurity", that I realized I was harboring the dangerous enemy in my house. He had crept in the back door and made himself very comfortable in my basement, filling my heart and home with toxic lies of insecurity.

Where does insecurity stem from? As women, we are surrounded with blaring messages to be a prettier, younger, better version of ourselves. I can only imagine the pressures the next generation of little girls we are raising will feel. Unfortunately, we live in a culture that tells us we are only as valuable as we are sensual. Women have about five minutes in the limelight and then we are thrown out as someone newer, younger, and skinnier takes our place. Meanwhile, we size up that woman, comparing ourselves with her and taking drastic measures with Botox, clothes, shoes, handbags, hair dye, and razors. As a result we sink deeper into our insecurities and build walls around ourselves. We lose our grip on reality, instead of living as God intended us to live.

Mind you, insecurity isn't just about our bodies. The early years of mothering were tough for me not just because I was a young mom, but because I wanted to be the best mom I could be for my baby. I wish I could go back to those first days of pregnancy and then Cheyenne's homecoming. Those memories are filled with heartache rather than joy. You see, I had listened to the lies and heard what everyone was telling me as truth.

"You won't be a good mother. You're only seventeen; consider abortion."

"Chris won't stay with you just because you're having his baby."

"Of course you missed the signs of her (Cheyenne's) reacting to the vaccines; you're a young mom."

"You can't be a good mom. You have to work and go to school."

Granted, your first days of meeting your newborn were much different than mine. (I truly hope for your sake.) Nevertheless, I'm sure insecurities plagued your thoughts. Should I breastfeed or not? Is it okay to give him another bottle; he just had one? How does Lucy make grocery shopping and caring for a newborn look so easy? Is this the right daycare for my baby? What if I make the wrong choice?

Because we live in a culture that values beauty and youth more than a person's heart, we will have the enemy in our faces telling us that we aren't the picture of perfection. If we are brave enough to confront this tactic head on, we'll find freedom. The truth is, we are not the picture of perfection, but we can reflect who God created us to be, and we can reflect the confidence we have in our relationship with Jesus.

When I wake up each morning, I lay there knowing I have two choices. I can choose to throw my doubts and caution to the wind and embrace God's truth, or I can listen to the lies the enemy is waiting to crush me with. We need to be aware and choose the truth—to choose God over what the world says is important. Beth Moore says in *So Long, Insecurity*, "Insecurity among women is epidemic, but it is not incurable. Don't expect it to go away quietly, however. We're going to have to let truth scream louder to our souls than the lies that have infected us."

The truth is found in the pages of my beloved Bible. During King Hezekiah's reign a war is looming. The truth in the words of his prayer stands the test of time.

> LORD, the God of Israel, enthroned between the cherubim, you alone are God over all the kingdoms of the earth. You have made heaven and earth. Give ear, LORD, and hear; open your eyes, LORD, and see; listen to the words Sennacherib has sent to ridicule the living God. (2 Kings 19:15-16)

King Hezekiah was in a desperate situation. He had received word that the brutal king of Assyria was coming after his kingdom. The enemy had sent a letter stating that Hezekiah's God would not save his kingdom. Not only had the enemy, Sennacherib, made threats to wipe out the entire kingdom, he also was mocking God. Because our God is a living God, He heard Hezekiah's prayer. That night the Lord sent an angel and wiped out 185,000 men in the Assyrian camp. Sennacherib tucked tail and ran home. Before another invasion could happen, his own sons assassinated him.

God alone holds the tools we need to fight our battles with insecurity. He never intended for us to fight this battle on our own. Our identity and security rest in Him. In *Every Name of God in the Bible*, Larry Richards writes, "Because God is the living God, we can rely on Him completely. We can face our challenges courageously, and we can freely appeal to Him when we are in need."

Even though I know this, insecurity in who I am is still my biggest stumbling block. Every time I think I have it licked, something or someone triggers my insecurities. You would think that a girl with a name that means "a flowering shrub that grows in rocky places" would have a knack for being able to suppress insecurities and flourish. Sadly, no. My life verse reminds me to look to God and to lift up my worries, insecurities, and concerns to the One who can bless me and fill me with confidence and peace.

> And why do you worry about clothes? See how the flowers of the field grow. They do not labor or spin. Yet I tell you that not even Solomon in all his splendor was dressed like one of these. (Matthew 6:28-29)

Just like learning how to jog at a steady pace, telling myself the truth of who I am is something I practice daily. If I pick up the pace and ignore what my body is telling me, I stumble and fall. The same goes with resting in God's Word. Daily I listen to what He tells me in His love letter (Bible) to me:

- I am God's child (John 1:12).
- I am Christ's friend (John 15:15).
- I belong to God (1 Corinthians 6:20).
- I have not been given a spirit of fear, but of power, love, and self-discipline (2 Timothy 1:7).
- I am assured all things work together for good (Romans 8:28).
- I have been established, anointed, and sealed by God (2 Corinthians 1:21-22).
- I am confident that God will perfect the work He has begun in me (Philippians 1:6).
- I am given God's glorious grace lavishly and without restriction (Ephesians 1:5, 8).
- I have redemption (Titus 2:14).
- I am forgiven (Colossians 1:14).
- I have purpose (Ephesians 1:9-11).
- I have hope (Jeremiah 29:11-12).
- I am included (Ephesians 1:13).
- I am secure (Ephesians 2:20).
- I am a dwelling for the Holy Spirit (Ephesians 2:22).
- I share in the promise of Christ Jesus (Ephesians 3:6).
- God's power works through me (Ephesians 3:7).
- I can approach God with freedom and confidence (Ephesians 3:12).

My insecurities threatened to fill every part of my life until El Chay reminded me that I need to rest in who I am as a woman and as a child of God. The Bible is the only tool that uproots these feelings and helps me to focus on the truth. Through the Scriptures above, feel what your spirit is telling you as you turn the pages of your Bible. Does a Scripture jump off the page, illuminating itself just for you? My friend, that is God's way of saying that verse is for you! Take it to heart, cherish it, memorize it, and rest in it!

Each day is a new day to rest in who He created us to be and to use the tools. He has given us of friendship, fellowship, prayer, and Scripture to combat what our world tells us. If we aren't careful to clean up the pandemic that insecurity has caused in our generation of women, it will tear apart the next generation we are trying to raise up.

As long as we are on this earth, insecurity is going to plague us and attempt to hide itself in our basements disguised as a friend. As a mother of two daughters, I am learning to be careful in how I react to a skinny woman with implants or yet another woman who seems to have more bling than me. (Note: I'm not biased against implants. I'd honestly like a pair but then it goes against learning to accept myself. For those who think implants are stupid, I apologize. Obviously being able to breastfeed from my lap is an accomplishment in your eyes—but not mine.) The more comfortable I am in myself, the more my daughters will pick up my security. Each day there is an opportunity to turn a blind eye to the ads we see on TV for makeup or weight loss. And each time, I turn to God, reminding myself and my girls we are God's perfect creations. If I can teach them to rest in their identity in God and to battle their insecurities with His help, I've done the best thing possible.

Mama's Time-Out

- Today, rest in God's truth of who you are. Take some time to journal about your own insecurities. What are the roots? Ask El Chay to give you the strength and grace to fight this battle so that you may rest in His truth and become the woman He intends for you to be.

- Looking for ways to combat insecurity? Take note of the Scriptures I referenced earlier in the chapter. Depending on your insecurity, use a Scripture verse to fill your heart with truth.

- Remember that God created you to be uniquely you and thank Him.

Today's Love Note

I praise you because I am fearfully and wonderfully made;
your works are wonderful,
I know that full well.
Psalm 139:14

I Call Him By Name

El Chay, I thank You that I can go to You in my time of need. No hurt is too small; no trouble is too great. And thankfully, no issue is too petty to bring to

You either. Help me to reach out to other women to create friendships in Your name instead of drawing conclusions based on the enemy's lies. Your Word says we house within us the living God. I ask that You examine my heart and expose my insecurities. Help me work through them, Lord, so that I may be confident in who I am as Your child. Thank You, Lord, for Your willingness to battle on my behalf. In Your mighty name, Amen.

YAHWEH SHAMMAH

The Lord Is There

Ezekiel 48:35

*Trust in the Lord with all your heart
and lean not on your own understanding;
in all your ways submit to him,
and he will make your paths straight.*

Proverbs 3:5-6

He Is There

"I'm so sorry, Amber. I just don't see a heartbeat. It's gone," the doctor said quietly as a few tears ran down her face. Amber wiped her own tears as she called her husband and made arrangements for her other kids so she could go to the hospital that evening to deliver her third unborn child. This time it was a girl just barely seventeen weeks along. Earlier in the year she had observed the day of her son Josiah's passing. She couldn't help but feel anxious over this pregnancy. It also didn't help that she had recently been diagnosed with Lupus Disease.

Later that evening, as Amber heard the cries of a mother and baby being united in the next room, she gave birth to her daughter, Cadyn. Surrounded by her close friends and husband, they marveled at how perfect she was and how she already resembled her living siblings. She held Cadyn in her hands, took pictures, and prayed over her body. Amber was strangely at peace. She was able to laugh and mourn all in the same breath because God's presence filled her room. The Lord, Yahweh Shammah, was there.

Yahweh Shammah is a name that is actually reserved for a city. However, it's not just a city. "The Lord Is There" because His presence is there. He was there for Amber when she carried her precious babies, just as He was there when she didn't see her baby's heartbeat on the screen. He was there when she gave birth, and He was there in the dark hours afterward as Amber tried to sleep on the maternity ward listening to the cries of joy and pain of other mothers and to the babies whose lives had just begun.

Amber's children were her life, and this pregnancy was a sign of hope after losing two babies. But Amber had an anchor. Her rope was firmly tied to her mighty God, and she hung on with all the strength He supplied. She knew if she lost her faith she truly would lose everything.

If we lose God, we lose hope, love, kindness, protection, goodness, strength, wonder, justice, and grace. We lose faith; we lose God. The worst pain anyone can ever feel is losing a child. Losing God in the process is like losing a lifeline to heal that pain.

Take a few minutes today and imagine what life would be like without Him. What would life be like for your children without Him?

Pain and suffering are a part of life. While this may be hard to swallow, there is wisdom in being able to embrace this thought. The Bible says there will be pain and trials of many kinds for those who believe in Christ. If we are not careful, this pain can damage our faith and render us defenseless. But if we choose to praise God in the midst of it all, He will receive it for His glory.

Amber was able to make it through her miscarriage and stillbirth because she didn't turn away from Him. Though she was angry and hurt, she reached out to her Father God for comfort and praised Him that her daughter was so perfectly formed. She was also able to thank God that her little Cadyn would never know the suffering of this life. Instead she was in heaven laughing and playing with her two brothers and walking side by side with Jesus.

The questions "Why?" and "How come?" were in the back of my mind as I walked with Amber in her journey of loss. At the time, I didn't understand why God would allow this to happen. I think each woman who experiences loss comes to her own conclusions with God while she walks through her darkest days.

I remember sitting on the edge of the pool watching Elijah tread through his swimming lessons when the subject of more kids arose. Jen and Aliisa asked me if I wanted more children. As always, I laughed and replied, "I'd love more, but it's so hard to conceive. God is in charge of my uterus." August 8, 2011, marked the day we learned we were expecting our fourth baby. I was astonished and so thankful. Within days of learning we were pregnant, I posted on Facebook, "If you want to make God laugh, tell Him your plans. Riggleman Baby 4.0 will arrive in April 2012."

The emotions of expecting another baby whirled from excitement to feeling overwhelmed. Could I raise another baby? Do I have too much on my plate? Lord, I need Your help! Even though I was excited, something gnawed at my mind. I couldn't put my finger on it, but something wasn't right about this pregnancy. As the weeks passed by, my Sonrise Bible study sprang back into session with new faces and new seating assignments. I was assigned to sit next to Halley. She had just moved to Kearney and was showing off her latest addition, Abraham. When we asked about her life experiences, she opened up about her miscarriages. Immediately, her stories of loss connected with my heart. It was as if the Holy Spirit was trying to help me prepare for what I would learn the following day.

Halley had difficulties getting pregnant. After her first early miscarriage, several months later, God blessed her with twin girls. Later, when they tried for another child, she thought she could breathe a sigh of relief as she entered into her third trimester. Yet, she lost her little boy when she was nearly seven months pregnant. She talked about the darkness she walked through and how God allowed her relationship with Him to be tested to the max. "But I came out on the other side of my grief walking more closely and intimately with God."

As I shoved the uneasiness to the back of my mind, I couldn't shake the feeling that somehow that moment of listening to her journey was meant for my heart. As I lay in bed that night, thoughts of Amber and Halley came to my mind.

I never really understood the depth of God's strength and His love for me until the following morning. I went to my ultrasound appointment full of joy, anticipating my baby's thunderous heartbeat on the screen. As I lay there, the doctor became silent as my womb filled the monitor. She frowned as she moved the screen out of my sight before confirming my worst fears. My baby was gone. No heartbeat could be seen—no movement, no life. My worst fears were confirmed. God knew how hard it was for us to conceive and how we dreamed of another child. I kept thinking maybe it was a mistake and this moment wasn't happening.

During the dark hours of the day, all I could do was grieve for my baby and what could have been. I questioned God. I longed to hear His voice, to feel His healing touch, to be pulled in to His presence. As I lay there grieving, I heard Him tell me it's in the brokenness that He brings healing. His hands were already there to mend my heart.

He reminded me that it's in the times that we are hurting or fallen from grace that He is there. Under the weight of our pain, He brings peace in some tangible way. Yet at the same time, I was angry. Angry that He allowed my child to die. I wanted so badly to stand in His presence, to rail my fists against His chest, and to question why. I was so tired of pretending that I understood His will and what was best for me. I wanted to shed the walls surrounding my emotions and be real. I wanted to question if He would still be there for me in the midst of my pride, anger, and ugliness. I was tired of pretending it was alright and pretending that I would be fine.

In those dark hours, all I could hear was the love He has for me. Over and over He told me that His love surrounds us when we are broken from the pain. He is carrying us as we reel from the anger and turn it toward Him. It's in those moments that He loves us all the more. Our hearts are so precious to Him. He asks us to hand over our lives, our pain, our hearts in an understanding that we need Him. And when we surrender, He gives us solace.

The sharp knife of a short life cuts deep as it breaks our hearts. We grieve the dreams and future we had already planned, but He is there in the heartache. In the midst of the storm, He comforts us and never forsakes us. As the dark days faded into new days, God whispered in the midst of my pain that He was still there.

The words of Ezekiel 48:35 hold hope and truth for our hurting hearts. "And the name of the city from that time on will be: THE LORD IS THERE." As Ezekiel spoke these words, he was foretelling the birth of Christ. He not only proclaimed words of truth, he gave words of hope. He gave the people in that day and age something real to cling to. Now, more than two thousand years later, His words give hope to someone like Amber, Halley, and myself. Through His Word, Yahweh Shammah brings His Spirit. He is there. We can take shelter and know that it's where our hurting heart and unanswered questions belong.

Mama's Time-Out

- Losing a child is something no one should ever experience, yet many do. The pain fades but our hearts bear the scars. It's in God's arms that our hearts are mended. Ask God to mend yours.

- If you've lost a child, take some time to remember your little one and do something in honor of him or her. Whether your child was ten weeks in gestation or four years old, honor him. It could be as simple as sharing memories or letting go balloons on the day of his passing. Remember, little mama, your child is forever in your heart and in God's hands. The day you meet your Maker is the day you will be reunited with your child.

- My children had a difficult time comprehending that our baby was no longer in my tummy but in heaven. One of the ways we helped them understand was my reading the book, *Heaven Is For Real* by Todd Burpo.

The author's son Colton visited heaven and met his older sister who had died through a miscarriage.

Today's Love Note

When you pass through the waters,
I will be with you;
and when you pass through the rivers,
they will not sweep over you.
When you walk through the fire,
you will not be burned;
the flames will not set you ablaze.

Isaiah 43:2

I Call Him By Name

Father God, I praise Your name that I am able to call You Yahweh Shammah. You are there when I hurt; You are there when I grieve. You know the trials I have faced and walked through. It's a comfort to know that You have been and will be there through it all. Thank You for Your grace, Your comfort, Your goodness. Thank You most of all that You are there. Amen.

So Be It

Life holds a fragile web,
    its links are torn and broken
Often times, it gives away and pain becomes
    the token.
Yet through the pain
    we find the core of courage in the heart.
We build again what life has blown apart.
No easy task confronts us now
    as one by one
We weave the tangled memories of love
    which we so dimly perceive
    back together again.
And through the weeping in our souls
    the web grows strong again
And life begins to whisper . . . Amen

Lois Tiffany © Christianartsongs.blogspot.com/2009/04/sobeit.html

The Lord Is There, Too

The pain of losing a child never goes away. It ebbs and flows in our daily existence. For me, it has died down to a quiet roar. Knowing that the Lord is here eases the pain in my heart. My youngest often asks, "Mom, is the baby in your tummy in heaven with Jesus?"

"Yes, darling she is."

Satisfied with my answer, she runs off to play with her My Little Pony's and Squinkies.

For my friend, Amber, missing the child she lost catches her heart in the most unexpected times. In the moments when no one is looking she will rub her belly, missing the life that once grew inside of her. Other moments that catch her breath are when her daughter, Grace, says, "Mom, I miss my sister." Amber replies that she does too as she smiles at her daughter in the backseat while secretly wiping away her tears.

Telling someone who has lost a child that the hurt will go away with time is almost an insult. The pain may diminish, but it will never disappear. My Aunt Dolly lost her sixteen-year-old son, Jimmy, nearly eighteen years ago. She will be honest and say the pain is still there. At times, she still expects her son to walk through the door.

It seems that Amber, Dolly, and I have no one to turn to who really understands what our hearts are feeling. Yes, there are other mothers who have lost children, but each mother who faces loss walks through the valley of darkness on her own. It may be the same path, but each journey is different. In the midst of it, we wrestle with holding onto our grief and finally giving it to God.

It's been nearly six months since I lost my baby. Sometimes when I close my eyes, I wonder what she would have looked like. Would she have had my temper and my husband's compassion? Would she have been Tori's best friend?

The grief of losing a child isn't merely putting to rest her memory or the "what could have beens." Sometimes I question why it's so hard to let the dream of my beloved baby be laid to rest. If I let her go, lay her memory to rest, am I a bad mother, or will letting go allow me to move on with life again? Wrestling with my own grief can be compared to my hands acting as locks on cages. If I let it go, if I open the door, will God be there to take my hands and fill my heart with His healing?

Grief is one journey where we can all be sure we have a walking partner. God has been there, He understands the pain, the grief, and the loss. God knows the loss of a child. He sent His Son to earth for thirty-three years so that Jesus could walk among us. Though He was able to converse with His Son and watch Him grow, He also began to prepare His heart for the pain His only Son would endure. The Bible says the day that Jesus died, the heavens grew dark with thunderclouds. Darkness covered the earth in the middle of the afternoon. God could no longer bear to see His Son suffering, covered with sins He never committed.

What's even more difficult to comprehend is that God could have stopped it at any time.

He could have brought Jesus home the day He was hanging out at the Temple when He was twelve years old. God could have brought Him home after He was baptized by John. And He could have brought Jesus home before He was stripped, beaten, and nailed to that cross. However, God loves us just as much as He loves His Son, Jesus. The only way He could bring us home was to cover our sins with Jesus' blood as an atonement and sacrifice. Yes, God knows the pain of seeing a child die.

The Lord was there when Amber lost her child. The Lord was there when the news was given to my Aunt Dolly that her son had rolled his truck. God was there waiting for me when the ultrasound showed my baby's heart was not beating. The Lord is there during those moments when our little one comes to mind. The

Lord is present during our pain. He knows that losing a child is never easy. After all, He sacrificed His only Son to bring us home.

Mama's Time-Out

- The pain of losing a child is great and the sting never fully fades. If you know a friend who is grieving over losing a child, be brave enough to offer her support while she is hurting. Listen with compassion while she talks about her loss and remember, silence is okay, too. All that needs to be said is simply, you are sorry. Offer other practical ways to help her during her time of loss. Grocery shop, prepare a casserole meal, ask friends to help fill her freezer for a week, walk the family pet, run errands, or take her out to lunch.

- Be sensitive and offer to do these things on the anniversary date of your friend's loss too.

Today's Love Note

The LORD is close to the brokenhearted and saves those who are crushed in spirit.
Psalm 34:18

I Call Him By Name

Lord, it gives so much comfort and strength to know You are there. Thank You for being there when I lost my child, and thank You for being there for each of us when we are grieving. As my sisters cry out to You, I pray that Your spirit and Your sacrifice becomes a healing balm for their hearts.

It heals my heart to know that You, the God of this universe, understand my pain. Thank You again, Lord, for sacrificing Your Son for me. I'm thankful to know that You always will be there in my time of need and that I can call You Yahweh Shammah. It is my prayer that each woman who reads this book will grow closer to You and that they will call Your name in their time of need because You are there. Amen.

MACHSEH

God Is My Refuge

2 Samuel 22:1-3; Nahum 1:7; Psalms 3; 9:9-10; 61:1-3; Proverbs 18:10

*Even youths grow tired and weary,
and young [moms] stumble and fall;
but those who hope in the Lord
will renew their strength.*

Isaiah 40:30-31

A Place of Refuge from the Kids, Please!

Today I'm writing to you from a place you might appreciate. It's cool and quiet. Harmony seems to flow throughout this tiny space. I can almost catch my thoughts . . . and then the banging on the door ensues while at the same time little fingers reach under the door.

"Give me five more minutes," I yell through the door. "Mommy needs to go potty!"

"But Mommy, I wanna drink. Tori took mine."

Shrills of injustice penetrate my once hidden sanctuary. Now that I've been found out, it's time to leave my resting place and go referee my children.

Days like today I call "black Thursdays." The morning started out with two crabby children who woke up nearly two hours earlier than usual. Then one of my babies pooped all over the bathroom floor and tub. Next was the frantic rush to get my oldest off to school. Her medication for attention deficit disorder still hadn't taken effect causing her to bounce from one place to another. In the meantime, I scrambled to get her dressed, fed, and into the mini-van. I piled Tori, Elijah, and three daycare kids into the van and maneuvered like a rocket through traffic to get Chy to school on time—in my jammies, no less.

As the day wears on, things take a turn for the worse. It's raining with a slight chance for tornados. Translation—all my children, including my three daycare kids, are confined to the basement of my home where untamable chaos and wars break out.

Naturally my husband calls to tell me he needs to travel out of town unexpectedly and will return home in three days. Once I get that message, I run to the bathroom sending up a much needed prayer. "Lord, You know I love my children and love being home—but I can't stand my children right now. Please give me a moment of solace and refuge in You. Help me to be patient before I throw them and myself into the path of that tornado!"

The day wore on and God answered my prayers, giving me just enough patience to make it to five o'clock with the kids. I was exhausted but thankful God was there when I needed Him. As each unexpected and frustrating event occurred, I could hear Him say to take a deep breath and remember He is there, right beside me, giving me the strength and refuge I needed.

In the Bible God is often mentioned and called upon as a strong tower, a dwelling place, a place of refuge. King David referred to God as a place of refuge when the circumstances he faced were too much to bear. The metaphor of God as a stronghold, a fortress, or a place of refuge was in relation to how cities were built with walls surrounding them to protect against invasions from enemies. Not only were walls built for protection, towers known as strongholds were built inside the cities where defense and resistance could continue if the walls fell.

In *Every Name of God in the Bible*, Larry Richards writes, "While the fortress cities of the ancient world provided security against raiding enemies, a determined and powerful foe could take the strongest fortress. Siege engines battered the walls. Fires were set to weaken the limestone out of which the walls were built. Often ramps of dirt and stone were constructed that reached the top of a city's walls and over which an invading army might advance. While earthly fortresses offered some security, however great a city's walls might be, the only true security a believer could find was in God" (79).

King David regularly looked beyond his city to God in whom he ultimately placed all his trust. God delivered him several times from his enemy, King Saul, and many more times from other enemies who opposed him and his God. Although David had many issues of his heart in which he sinned, he still turned to God for rest, comfort, and refuge.

On days like "black Thursdays" when our enemies seem to be the sweet faces of our children, God provides a place of refuge. We find it by resting in the knowledge that no matter how great or small the battle, or how familiar or friendly we are with the current enemy, He is strong enough to carry us. All we have to do is put our trust in Him. God has placed His walls of love around us and will barricade us from the onslaught of attacks if we choose to look over the walls directly to Him for help, guidance, and refuge. He is our refuge from something as simple as feeling overwhelmed with our children, to attacks from a bigger enemy when it comes to our hearts and vulnerabilities.

Mama's Time-Out

- King David wrote many psalms referring to God as his place of refuge, as his strong tower. Take a moment today and flip through them to find a psalm that applies to your situation. Then pray that psalm and thank God for His place of refuge... even if it is the bathroom for time-out!

- As impossible as it sounds, take at least five minutes to yourself each day. Then, if you can arrange it, swap kids with a friend once a month so you can have some ME time. Use it to honor God as your refuge and to relax!

Today's Love Note

*Be my rock of refuge, to which I can always go;
give the command to save me,
for you are my rock and my fortress.*
Psalm 71:3

I Call Him By Name

Machseh, who can I go to when I am stressed, when I feel tired, when I feel like I can't take it anymore? Who can I run to when situations in life rise up and overwhelm me? There is no one strong enough to protect me and bring peace. Thank You, Machseh, that You are with me. I pray each day that I can find my refuge in You. Thank You that I can go to You—that You are my place of refuge. There is no one like You, God. Thank You for these moments when I can restore my strength by turning to You. Amen.

You Are My Strong Tower

"Okay, Heather, don't push, don't move, don't even sneeze!" my nurse commanded as calmly as possible as she pulled her gloves off after checking to see if my son was anywhere near the birth canal. Nearly nineteen hours after being induced, my son was crowning without me feeling the sensation of pressure or contractions thanks to a strong epidural. The nurse didn't tell me the cord was bulging its way out next to his head and his heart rate was becoming erratic.

Within seconds, my doctor was in the room still in her pajamas, cutting me from one end to the other to make room for his head. At the same time, she was pushing the cord back in. The room was full of tension; the nurses barely breathed while prepping the crash cart. My husband's face said it all as he watched his son slither out blue and barely breathing. The cord had been wrapped around his neck. Each contraction had pinched off his oxygen supply.

I prayed sighs of relief as he meowed like a kitten and each cry became more lustful for air. Soon he was screeching. I held my golden-haired, blue-eyed bundle of cuteness as joy flooded my heart. After seven years of waiting, I was a new mother once again to my little Elijah. This mommy was on cloud nine.

Days later the joy had subsided as my hormones began wreaking havoc on my emotions.

And the baby blues set in. Thinking that it would level out within a few days, I let it go, but the feeling of sadness and irritability continued. I thought it was just due to the stress of Elijah's birth and having to deal with his high levels of jaundice. We were in the clinic nearly every day for two weeks. I also had trouble with nursing. Elijah never seemed to wake up long enough to want to eat. When he did, it was barely two hours from the last feeding. I was on autopilot from the lack of sleep and the demands of new mothering on top of trying to balance my other pre-newborn commitments.

Nearly eight months passed until my husband, who refused to see the doctor unless he was sure he was dying, made me an appointment. By that point, I seldom left the house or got out of my pajamas, much less showered. The idea of going to a grocery store for something as simple as milk was like climbing Mount Everest in flip-flops. My doctor took one look at me and not only prescribed medication, she doubled the dose and told me it was time to stop breast-feeding before my hormones killed me by way of insanity.

I didn't understand why God would allow this, and I was miffed at the idea of taking medication and the fact that I was clinically depressed. It reminded me of the days when God brought me out of manic depression and healed me. Two years later I was too proud to be back to square one. When I spoke of my past trials with depression, I bragged that I was not taking medication because God had healed me. So why would He allow this to happen again? Why didn't He prevent it so I could enjoy the gift of my son I had begged and pleaded for? I was a committed, godly woman. I read my Bible and prayed daily. I couldn't make sense of it.

After beginning the dreaded regimen, I heard God whispering that I could not depend on myself. Instead, I needed to make Him my refuge, my strong tower. He was my Creator. Although I was fearfully and wonderfully made, my own hormones could be my means of destruction if I didn't accept the help He provided through modern-day remedies. Even though I'd rather have been healed instantly by faith like some of my favorite Bible characters, He had other ideas.

I had fallen on the notion that I was to be independent and strong. Like so many other American women, I swallowed the enemy's lies. Trained by the example of our own mothers and history, we believe we need to ponytail our hair and pull up our bootstraps (a.k.a. stiletto heels) as we independently and effortlessly run our households for all to see. Any help or strength we need as women, we learn to draw from within ourselves. For me, this time around, it was not going to work. I had no strength left. When I felt the weakest, I was drawn to begin searching for God's lesson in all of this.

When God is mentioned in the Bible, He is noted to dwell among His people. His names are all closely related and intertwined because God wants us to depend on nothing but Him as our Refuge, Shield, Fortress, Dwelling Place, and Strong Tower. Perhaps that is why David wrote so many psalms about God as his Strong Tower. (Plus, I believe that King David was one of those "emo" people. His own hormones and emotions messed with him. Don't believe me? Review the psalms. David was in touch with his feelings... or just plain touched.)

After years of running because his life was at stake thanks to King Saul (another touched man), David had to depend utterly and solely on God. His skill, wit, friends, or family could not save him from the king. David wrote, "Whoever dwells in the shelter of the Most High will rest in the shadow of the Almighty. I will say of the LORD, 'He is my refuge and my fortress, my God, in whom I trust'" (Psalm 91:1-2).

Thankfully, like David, God delivered me from my sadness when my hormones took me through a desert. As the days passed with my new medication regimen, I looked to God as my refuge, my safe place. Soon the days weren't dreary and the idea of going to the store for milk became a bright spot in my day. God was waiting for me to turn to Him and say, "God, you are my strong tower and I will run to You when nothing else makes sense. I will run to You for comfort, for strength. I will run to You when my hormones wage battle against me. I will trust in You alone."

Mama's Time-Out

- When do you run to God for refuge—in times of trouble or throughout each day?

- What reasons prevent you from running to Him or depending on Him? Embrace who He is and make the decision to run to Him for everything.

- How do you depend on God? Can you begin demonstrating to your children how you depend on God as your refuge? Build a fort in your living room and ask your kids how God is like that fort.

Today's Love Note

Hear my cry, O God;
listen to my prayer.
From the ends of the earth I call to you,
I call as my heart grows faint;
lead me to the rock that is higher than I.
For you have been my refuge,
a strong tower against the foe.

Psalm 61:1-3

I Call Him By Name

Lord, Your Word is filled with examples of how You have been a strong tower, a place of refuge, and a comfort to Your people. Help me to turn to You in all my times of trouble, whether great or small. Help me to keep my eyes ever on Your hands as You continue to hold my life in them. Open my eyes and turn my ears to You as I go about my daily task of raising the children You've loaned me. Amen.

ELOHIM

Creator

Genesis 1:1, 14, 22, 26-28; Deuteronomy 32:6;
Isaiah 40:28; 42:5; Matthew 19:4

Wonder

I wonder how the waves roll in
Is the face of God behind the wind?
Tell me why children like to spin?
These things I think I might ask him.
I wonder where and how and why
I wonder if the angels fly
I'm curious to know if I have spied
an angel on this side of life.

© Rachel Scott, Resolution Album 2008

You Created Me for This?

It's so refreshing to view the world through the eyes of a child. Things that were monotonous to us become brand new. Walking becomes a treasure hunt filled with exciting discoveries, smelling flowers becomes tantalizing to our senses, and touching snow is magical as we watch it melt in our child's hands. Responsibilities and maturity haven't caused them to abandon their curiosity and joy over the wonders of God's creation. They are in awe because the earth is full of His glory.

Think about it. Children are intrigued with the intricacies of a butterfly's wings and the size of an elephant's ears. They giggle in delight at the way grass tickles their feet and respect sticker patches. They love the colors that streak across the sky at sunset and marvel over the shapes they see in the clouds. They listen intently to the sound of a heartbeat before moving on to study our eyes and perform science experiments by poking them.

As a new mother of young children, it is so easy to become consumed with their demands and schedules and to forget about our Father God and everything else. Sleep deprivation sets our minds on autopilot. Our thoughts wander back to our previous job occupation. Compared to motherhood, it seemed like a vacation. But our children have a way of bringing us back to our Creator and reminding us of how we as women get to take part in His creation.

So what does God have to do with motherhood and childbearing? Everything! We have the privilege of sustaining life within us while God's hands are busy knitting together our little ones. Our intuition was created for more than just what we sense our boss needs in the boardroom or what our husband is hinting for in the bedroom. God has created us with an uncanny ability to know what a child needs with just a look. But some of us feel like we don't have these instincts, or so we think. We become nervous and question our abilities as we inhale books on babies and parenting.

Yet, no matter how unprepared you feel, you were given the ability to be a mother. Our genetic and spiritual design is just as intricate and remarkable as a snowflake or any other natural wonder. If you ask me, I'd say we are even more unique because of our ability to laugh and cry in the same breath, to sustain life, and to build up another person's heart.

Our connection to God becomes more intimate when we become mothers. We become more aware of the presence of Elohim as the world around us and the baby we hold in our arms speak of His presence. Elohim means Creator. He created billions of galaxies that we are just now discovering. He created the molecule Laminin that holds our bodies together. It's in the form of a cross, no less. (Type in Louie Giglio and Laminin on YouTube.) Every part of us and every bit of nature proclaims He is God and He is good. The earth is full of His glory!

Elohim is found on the very first pages of the Bible and is how God introduces Himself to us. When the Bible is translated from its Hebrew and Greek roots, Elohim is found over twenty-five hundred times and thirty-two times in the first chapter of Genesis, according to my favorite book of facts, *Every Name of God in the Bible* by Larry Richards. Elohim is the first name that gives us something tangible about God's character. It describes His ability to speak and light goes forth. It also establishes His sovereignty, creativity, and power. He is the Creator and the living God. I don't know about you, but this very thought gives me shivers as I look at the world around me.

God allows us to have children for various reasons, but I believe the main reason is to understand His heart and His love for us. No one else quite understands what it's like to have our hearts toddling outside our bodies except for God. Before He created the earth, He already knew about the choices Eve and Adam would make as well as the choices you and I would make. And yet He did it anyway because He had a plan. His plan was to give us a chance to love Him freely through the acceptance of His Son, Jesus, who was born as a man and yet was fully God.

Children are God's way of bringing us back to Him. As we grow up, we tend to have this uncanny ability to think the world revolves around us. I remember being so focused on my goals and my plans and how I always compared my achievements to others. It was easy to put God in a box and think that I had accomplished these things by my own abilities. But when that pregnancy stick shows two lines, suddenly our thinking begins to shift. The orbit that revolved around us suddenly orbits around our bellies as we devour every nacho and book in sight. Somehow our hearts have given way to the process of creation, and we have unknowingly fallen in love with Elohim.

After our children are born and we begin the task of feeding them and teaching them, we are again reminded of our mighty Creator. Our hearts are pricked by the emotions that well up within us for our newborn, and this connection reminds us of God and His Son. Our hearts are suddenly pricked again as we see the love expressed for us in every painted sunset or dimpled smile our baby gives us.

One day I sat listening to Rachel Scott sing about the wonders of this world and of God. My senses, though a bit fuzzy from lack of sleep, were refreshed as I took in the world around me. My children whirled in circles and giggled from the sensations they felt. I couldn't resist joining them in whirling and giggling. God is passionate for us. All we have to do is look out the window to see the good in the world He created for us. Our God surrounded us with the hand of His creation as a reminder of His love and to bring us back to Him when the world tries to pull our attention away.

I want to encourage you to pick up one of Rachel Scott's albums and listen to the words of "I Wonder." If your heart has been numb to His presence and you need a moment to be reminded and refreshed, go look through the eyes of your child. Take in the wonders that she sees. Elohim will become more than just a name to you.

Mama's Time-Out

- In life or nature, what reminds you of God? Smelling the fresh scent of rain on the earth or watching the sunrise? Talk to God and thank Him for the moments that take your breath away.

- Depending on the time of year, there are different ways to introduce God's handiwork to your kids. Take them to the zoo and point out the different works of His creation.

- Collect leaves with your children. Then use freezer paper, place the leaves under the paper, and have your child color over the top of the leaf on the paper. Compare the differences. Take a hike and encourage your kids to spot as many different creatures as they can and to praise God for them.
- Read them the story of creation, and then take turns sharing what they like best of God's creation.

Today's Love Note

Do you not know?
Have you not heard?
The LORD is the everlasting God,
the Creator of the ends of the earth.
He will not grow tired or weary,
and his understanding no one can fathom.
He gives strength to the weary
and increases the power of the weak.

Isaiah 40:28-29

I Call Him By Name

Elohim, thank You for my children. Thank You for letting me house Your mighty creation of my children. Help me to bring You glory through teaching them about You. It's amazing to think You know every hair on my head and that You took such care in creating me for the purpose of mothering my children. Please continue to give me strength when I am tired and to open my eyes to Your work all around me. I pray in Your wondrous name. Amen.

When I Grow Up

In the beginning, when Elohim laid the foundations of the earth, He had every single one of us in mind. As He called forth the light and threw the stars into the sky, He was thinking of us. When He created the Grand Canyon and the Sand Hills of Nebraska, He was thinking of us. When He chose where you would live and what you would look like, He was thinking of you.

The God of all creation got just a bit more creative when He began framing you. He thought about your character, your temperament, your eye color, your voice . . . He knit you together within your mother's womb, along with the dream He planted inside your heart. It may be dormant or hasn't surfaced yet. Or, like me, you may push your dreams out of your mind as you rock your little one back and forth. After all, what is more important than wiping noses, changing diapers, fixing suppers, and waiting in line at the car pool lane? It's everything, if you know how to balance motherhood, but it does not equal all of you.

Motherhood is a huge gift of nurturing someone you created out of love to experience life in the fullest. But that isn't all God created you to be. Mothering is only part of your identity; it's part of the role you serve.

I was excited to be the whole world to both my children, but motherhood wasn't in my dreams as a child. I dreamed of being a counselor or lawyer. (I'm an expert in arguing my point!) These dreams lay dormant in my heart for many years, especially after I had my first child. As a teen mother, something shifted within me when I first laid eyes on my baby. I wanted nothing more than to prove to everyone that though I was young, I was still a good mom.

The months passed and I was neck deep in bottles, diapers, drool, and the sweetest smiles. I had abandoned everything—a career, relationships, and social outings to be more focused on my child. But I felt a sense of emptiness; I was unfulfilled. If that shocks you, I apologize, but I want you to understand I felt there was something more out there. There was something more I was meant to do; and if I didn't find it, I was going to lose any sense of self. I loved motherhood, but it didn't work as my entire identity. There were pieces of me that still lay undiscovered.

Wearily as I laid my son down, a quiet voice nudged me to look in at the top shelf of the closet. There, nestled and buried amongst all the baby gear, were my journals. Writing had always come naturally to me and was my escape from everyday things. I often used it to encourage my friends with letters, poems, and stories. I dusted them off and laid them on my nightstand where I forgot about them until I read about Ordinary. Perhaps you've heard of him?

The Dream Giver by Bruce Wilkinson and David Kopp is about a man named Ordinary who discovers more to life than what he knew. Ordinary was a man who lived in the Land of Familiar who discovered the Dream Giver and the Big Dream that was planted in his heart. At the nudging of the Dream Giver, Ordinary sets out on a journey to find his dream. In the process he encounters criticism of all kinds from everyone—from his parents, his best friend, and even the mayor.

Yet, Ordinary chooses to follow his heart. Although he encounters many other obstacles, he doesn't give up. Accompanied at times by his friend, Faith, in the end his dream inspires other Nobodies and Somebodies to follow the Dream Giver.

The Dream Giver in this story is God, and the obstacles Ordinary faced are much like our own. Children aside, what other dreams did God plant inside your heart? What obstacles do you face? I faced obstacles of not knowing where to begin and how to share my heart with others. What about my babies? How would I find time to write? What was the purpose in all this? What was the point in sharing my story with small groups of women?

One day, everything changed. It's still etched in my memory when I found my purpose. I have my favorite group of mamas to thank. I call them my Sonrise Chica's. One morning at our Sonrise Bible Study I shared that I thought God wanted me to write. So with some encouragement, I began blogging and remained obedient to what I heard the Dream Giver telling me. One month later, as I cleaned up dried mac and cheese off the floor during nap time, I had an unexpected visitor. Our Bible study leader, Jean, stopped by to give me a love gift. As I opened the envelope, several twenty-dollar bills fell out. She then proceeded to tell me, with tears in her eyes, that it was in her heart as well as the hearts of the other forty-five girls from my Bible study group to help pave the way to the Colorado Christian Writers' Conference. I was speechless.

"Heather, you have a gift, and we feel that God wants us to help you seek it and use it," Jean said as she hugged me and left.

With encouragement from friends and family, we made it to the conference where my dreams were realized. God was not only using my experiences as a stay-at-home mother to raise my children, but He was using my gift to encourage other mothers.

Our dreams, abilities, and talents weren't fashioned just for our enjoyment. They are other pieces of the puzzle that make you, uniquely you. When we learn to use our abilities, life is so much sweeter. Suddenly the void within our hearts is gone because we are glorifying God through our giftings. Your talents may be much different from mine, but they all work together to benefit your children in every way. A friend of mine is a stay-at-home mom of six. She is quiet, very patient, loves to teach, and creative. This year she is homeschooling her oldest two children.

Elohim not only created you to raise your children, He also created you with another special purpose. How God our Creator, our Dream Giver, fashioned us is His gift to us. What we do with it is our gift to Him.

Mama's Time-Out

- Do you identify yourself totally as a mom?
- What dreams lie dormant in your heart?
- When you grow up, what do you want to be?
- The next time you introduce yourself to someone, say something like, "Hi I'm Heather, I'm a writer and a mom." Or, "I'm a runner and enjoy being a mother."

Today's Love Note

Then God said, "Let us make mankind in our image, in our likeness, so that they may rule over the fish in the sea and the birds in the sky, over the livestock and all the wild animals, and over all the creatures that move along the ground."
So God created mankind in his own image, in the image of God he created them; male and female he created them.

Genesis 1:26-27

I Call Him By Name

Elohim, help me to find breathtaking moments throughout my day when I look at the world You created. You could have created a world that is dull and gray, and yet You chose to dazzle me every day. Remind me to thank You for the birds that sing and the fresh air I breathe. I thank You that Your miracles didn't stop there. I thank You for creating me with a special purpose in mind. I thank You for the gifts You've given me. Help me to discover in my heart the dream that You planted. Help me to pursue You in that dream and all that I do. Amen.

EL SHADDAY

Almighty God

Genesis 17:1-2; 35:11; 48:3; 49:25; Psalm 90

*Against all hope,
Abraham in hope believed and so became the father of many nations,
just as it had been said to him, "So shall your offspring be."*

Romans 4:18

Nothing Is Impossible with Him

Where does a woman turn when all of her friends are seemingly able to get pregnant with ease or carry a child to term? I wasn't so sure myself as I flung my Bible on the floor. I stared at the ceiling as the tears slid down my face. My best friend, Angela, was now pregnant with baby number two. As for me, I was still waiting. It had been nearly seven years since the birth of my first child, Cheyenne. I was beginning to think that God had closed my womb. Was this punishment for my past behavior and mistakes when I wasn't living a life for Him? I was more than devastated.

Cheyenne was a "fluke" that happened my senior year of high school. I knew I should be content that I had her. Still, the desire to have another child filled my thoughts and haunted my sleep. I gave careful consideration to diet, exercise, vitamins, sleep, and stress—not to mention positions, timing, charting, temperature taking, and the list went on. Still, each month Mother Nature showed up with her lovely gift.

After seeing the doctor, the news we received zapped any hope of having another child. My doctor listed several reproductive disorders and stated it was unlikely I would conceive again on my own. The icing on the cake was being required to go through a humiliating process in which my husband and I did the baby dance and scrambled to my doctor's office within an hour of the deed. From there, she scooped out my insides to scrutinize under the microscope. It seemed at least six other personnel besides my doctor knew why I was there. Embarrassment barely describes how I felt, but it gave me hope that conceiving could be possible. People from the check-in counter to those who worked in the lab seemed to eyeball me and say, "I know what you just did—the baby dance!"

The final shock were the words the doctor uttered after playing with her microscope. "It is unlikely you will conceive on your own. Heather, I'm going to be frank. Your environment is too hostile for your husband's swimmers. You do not ovulate every cycle, and your luteal phase is defective. Add these complications to your scarred fallopian tubes, tilted uterus, and endometriosis, it's a miracle you conceived your daughter. We can try several rounds of fertility drugs before we move on to insemination, but I want to caution you, it may not work."

Can a women's body be described as hostile? I thought to myself. I was more than hostile when the news sank into my heart that I would have to undergo fertility treatments that might not even work. It was discouraging to know that because of the cost of the procedures, we would need to wait a few more years before we could afford such treatment. The hopes I had to conceive another child seemed to dissolve.

Each night as my husband and I tucked our daughter in, she prayed that God would send her a brother to play with. Each night, I also prayed that God would open my womb for such a gift. His silence left me with a broken heart yearning for another baby.

So where does a woman turn? Some turn to other doctors, research different treatments, or reach out to their friends for comfort. I turned to my Bible and searched out all the women of the Bible who were barren. Not only did I find several stories, I stumbled across Scriptures that talked about a God for "whom nothing was impossible." It raised my interest, especially since it was near impossible to have a baby on my own. I needed a God who makes all things possible.

When we pray to El Shadday, we invoke the name "God Almighty." A closer inspection of the name in Hebrew means, "God the Mountain One." What is stronger and more unchanging than a mountain? What thoughts does it summon when you think about our God, our Creator, as a mountain?

The first time God is called El Shadday is in the story of Abram and Sarai. "When Abram was ninety-nine years old, the Lord appeared to him and said, 'I am God Almighty; walk before me faithfully and be blameless. Then I will make my covenant between me and you and will greatly increase your numbers'" (Genesis 17:1-2). Abram fell facedown and had a conversation with God that went something like this.

"What? Are you kidding me? I'm an old man, nearly a century old, and now you're going to tell me I'm going to have children?"

"What, you doubt Me? Let me repeat My name for you and remind you of the promise I made you. I AM GOD ALMIGHTY, nothing is impossible for Me. I have a plan, and timing is everything, My friend."

At this Abram chuckles and scratches his beard. "But God, Sarai is ninety years old. How can she be a mother? Her years of childbearing are past."

"You know what? You will give her the name Sarah for she will give you a son and you both will be the mother and father of many generations. You'll have so many descendants, it will be impossible to count them. It will be like trying to count the grains of sand on the shore. This is how I will show My glory and give hope for generations to come."

"Okay, so You have a plan, a couple of new names for us, and You're telling me that You are God Almighty. Can You do me a favor and let my son Ishmael live under this blessing, too?"

"Abram, like I said, I have a plan. Trust in Me that nothing is impossible. I will bless your faith."

Of course, Abram told his ninety-year-old wife the news and she too chuckled. But then her belly began to grow, and she began to feel life within her. She gave birth at the age of ninety-one to a son, her promised one.

In response to this story, I continued to hope in God, day in and day out. I knew that He would somehow display His glory in my life. I thought God knew what He was doing. As I prayed, I heard the answer I never expected.

"Delight yourself in Me, and I will grant the desires of your heart."

I began focusing on God's will for my life and laid the desires of my heart on His altar. The journey wasn't easy. I almost gave up all hope as I kept asking El Shadday to one day grant the desires of my heart.

Then the God of the impossible made everything possible. Over two years later, I felt tired and sluggish at work. I commented in passing to one of my girlfriends that my chest was sore. She teased me and stated that maybe I was pregnant. I shrugged it off until I got home and confided in my husband. Not even fifteen minutes later, we were in the feminine hygiene aisle comparing pregnancy tests at our local Walgreens store. We were elated as all five test sticks indicated that I was pregnant. Six months later our son was born and my prayers as well as my daughter's were answered.

While God doesn't always work in this fashion when it comes to infertility, don't give up hope. There is unquestionably nothing impossible that He cannot do. Against all odds, I now have three miracles that demonstrate the faith I have in my God.

He may answer your prayers by means of adoption or foster children, however, don't give up your faith. No matter how life may try to kill your dreams of being a mother, no power on earth or in heaven can thwart His plan for you as long as you follow our Almighty God.

Mama's Time-Out

Get a note card and write out the Scripture Psalm 37:4, "Take delight in the Lord, and he will give you the desires of your heart." Then ask yourself what keeps you from believing in God. What keeps you from believing He can make the impossible happen? Go to God and tell Him what is on your heart.

Today's Love Note

Take delight in the LORD, and he will give you the desires of your heart.
Commit your way to the LORD; trust in Him.
Psalm 37:4-5

I Call Him By Name

Father God, I love calling on Your Almighty name. How is it that the God of the universe cares so much about the desires of my heart? El Shadday, thank You for Your Word and for the lives of Sarah and Abraham. Help me to dwell in Your Word when my hope feels dashed upon the rocks. Help me to call on Your mighty name. Help me to remember that nothing is impossible for You. Amen.

He Keeps His Promises

As a mom, I've broken more than my fair share of promises to my children. What hurts the most is even after their initial disappointment, they still believe I'm a hero. This fact always sends me on a guilt trip. Try as I might to never break a promise, I've learned *not* to say, "I promise." Instead, I say, "I'll try."

Promises are words that create a bond between you and someone else. They imply hope, trust, and completion. They are a way of making someone's heart and soul feel safe. It can be a promise to get the laundry done, a promise to make sure there is gas in the van, a promise to be home on time from work, or a promise to make it to your child's game. All these promises have good intentions, but they are ultimately defective because promises come from mere human beings. Human beings are born flawed. We are known to make mistakes. We stumble and fall, and we break promises. We've been cursed since the fateful fall of Adam and Eve. (That reminds me of the chat I want to have with *both* of them when I enter the pearly gates.)

There is only one Person who has kept all His promises. Even thousands of years later, the words He has spoken are still coming true. God Almighty made promises throughout the Old and New Testament. From the beginning, God intervened, promising to forgive, protect, provide, and redeem us all through a Savior. His promises apply to every need we have. El Shadday is often translated not only as God of the mountains but also as The All Sufficient One. The Bible is full of His promises. Do you need some examples to teach your children, or do you need a fresh perspective of what He has promised?

His Word promised to send a Savior. He has promised to come back for us. He promised David that his kingdom would be established forever. He promised Noah to never flood the entire earth again. He even promised Elijah and the woman who helped Elijah that He would provide. Here are some other examples that you can look up.

- He promises to be with us and sustain us when we are afraid (Genesis 28:15; Deuteronomy 31:8; Psalm 50:15; Luke 21:17-18; James 4:8).
- He promises to guide all our decisions. No matter how simple or tough, we can look to the Bible for His answer (Psalm 32:8; John 8:12; Philippians 4:6-7; James 1:5).
- He promises to help us through any temptation (1 Corinthians 10:13; 2 Thessalonians 3:3).
- He promises to care for us when we are having a bad day, a really bad day (Isaiah 41:10; Matthew 11:28-30).
- He promises He has a plan for our future (Jeremiah 29:11).
- He promises to forgive and purify a truly repentant heart (2 Corinthians 7:10; 1 John 1:9).
- He promises to care for all of our needs (Luke 12:31; John 14:14; 1 John 5:14-15).

My dear little mama, today I invite you to put your trust in God Almighty. I invite you to speak His name. He is by your side, and it's in His nature to bless and care for the ones He loves.

Very recently, I too felt as though God had abandoned me. I felt alone and isolated. Little did I realize He had orchestrated a series of events to cause me to fully rely on Him. It was His way of showing me life is fleeting and always changing, but He is always there. He never changes, and He is sufficient to care for all my needs.

One Sunday during worship, the congregation was invited to come to the altar. While the music played, I heard Him say, *"Come."* After a moment of hesitation, I felt drawn to the altar where I sat barefoot on the floor with my palms lifted up as an offering to Him. Moments later, another set of hands were holding mine up in the midst of worshipping God and His precious Son, Jesus.

A flood of promises came as did His presence. He spoke through my dear friend whom I hadn't seen in months who had no idea of my struggles. She told me God had not abandoned me; I was not alone. He is always with me.

He stripped me of my family and friends so I could be refined in this desert period to rely more on Him. I came away from His presence that morning knowing that no matter the struggle or difficulty, He keeps His promises. That, my little mama, is sometimes how the Almighty moves and refreshes us with His presence and promises.

Perhaps you've not felt His presence in a while, and it feels as though you are walking in a desert with no end in sight. During your time in this vast wilderness, remember God has not abandoned you. He is with you, just as He didn't abandon His people when He led them out of Egypt or His Son when He was in the desert for those forty long days. Take time to rest in the shadow of the Almighty and stand on His promises. He will be your strength as you learn to trust in Him in the days and months to come. Rest in His promise for His Word cannot be broken.

Mama's Time-Out

- What Scriptures listed resonate with your heart?

- Take one or two Scriptures listed above and memorize them so they will come to mind when you need them the most. Teach them to your kids at the dinner table, too.

Today's Love Note

*Hear my prayer, LORD God Almighty; listen to me, God of Jacob.
Look on our shield, O God;
look with favor on your anointed [mamas].
Better is one day in your courts than a thousand elsewhere. . . .
LORD Almighty, blessed is the [mother] who trusts in you.*

Psalm 84:8-10, 12

I Call Him By Name

Thank You, El Shadday, for Your words of promise. I praise You even more for Your Word made flesh in Your Son, Jesus. Please reveal Yourself to me and remind me of Your promises as I walk through this desert place. Thank You for Your promises, and help me as I go about my day to demonstrate Your love to my children. Amen.

EL OLAM

The Everlasting God

Genesis 21:32-33

*Even to your old age and gray hairs I am he,
I am he who will sustain you.
I have made you and I will carry you;
I will sustain you and I will rescue you.*

Isaiah 46:4

When Nothing Else Seems to Last

"Heather . . . Sis, stop crying!" my brother said, exasperated. I sobbed even harder, letting my head rest on the window ledge of his truck. He was probably afraid he would end up drowning in his truck and never make it out of town alive.

"But I'm going to miss you so much. It's not going to be the same here anymore; you won't be just down the street," I whimpered as my tears flowed freely.

My youngest brother, Davey, had moved into our house four years ago after I was awarded custody of him. Being only nine years older than Davey made it difficult for me to fill the role of mother, especially when his friends would comment how "hot" I was. The worst embarrassment for the poor deviant was when I would be mistaken as his girlfriend during parent-teacher conferences.

Even though I held the keys to his freedom and loved acting as a big sis, I eventually had to come up with some sort of leverage in terms of who was boss. I resorted to threatening him with a cooking spoon. Seriously, all I had to do was pull the spoon out of its metal canister and the noise would send that boy running out the door. (His wife asked me as a wedding favor to never threaten or use my big spoons when they are over for supper.)

"Heather, you did your job. I'm all grown up now. You've turned me from an atheist anarchist to a warrior for God. Your time with me is done, and it's time for me to move on," Davey said in his best manly voice as he tried to keep my tears from flooding into his seat. He was indeed grown up. He was now married and had made a big decision to go back to Wyoming to mend things with our mother and stepfather. I was more than proud of that kid (more like a man-child), yet the emptiness I felt ached even more as I watched Davey and his wife, Jenna, drive away. Much had changed in the last three months. My brother's departure was the straw that broke this mama's back.

Change is something we mamas definitely understand more than anything. It is constant as our children grow from tiny sleeping infants to boisterous children. Davey's time with us was just another example of the constant change we all experience. He went from a confused, hurt teenage boy with more than a few issues to serving our King.

With life's seasons ever changing as well as the stages of mothering, what can we count on to be the same? Is there anything out there that will be the same today as it was yesterday and will be in the future? Yes! My ever-constant is God. The name El Olam in Hebrew means God has no beginning and no end. He's the Alpha and the Omega. It means that God is constant, steady, never changing. A day in His courts is like a thousand years to us.

We can turn to Him when we wonder where those years have gone with our little ones. We can turn to Him when we wonder what is happening in our world. More notably, we can turn to Him when it seems like our lives have crumbled overnight. He is aware of our need for something steady, constant, and unchanging. He is the only constant. Of the thousands of years our little ball we enduringly call Earth has spun around the sun, only one thing has remained the same—God. His plans, His love, His promises, His laws, and His compassion for us are still the same as they were yesterday and will remain the same tomorrow and the next day.

The Bible is full of this promise and constant. From the first to the last page, God is referred to as "eternal." The first time I saw this, I wondered what it really had to do with me—a mom in the twenty-first century.

There is a story in Genesis of a treaty Abraham made with a man named Abimelek about a watering well that was seized by Abimelek's servants. Because something like this could have started a war, and because Abimelek knew that God's hand strongly rested on Abraham, he made a wise choice to call for peace.

After the treaty had been made at Beersheba, Abimelek and

Phicol the commander of his forces returned to the land of the Philistines. Abraham planted a tamarisk tree in Beersheba, and there he called on the name of the LORD, *the Eternal God. (Genesis 21:32-33)*

How compelling it was to read that Abraham called God "The Eternal God," not just because of the treaty over the well but maybe because of the roller coaster ride he endured prior to the moment at the well. Just when old Abe thought things would remain constant and he would be growing old with his wife, he became a father. God also revealed to him that he would be the father of many nations and have descendants from both sons for years to come. Through life's roller coaster ride and Abimelek's motion for peace, Abraham felt God's hand of peace on him. Abraham was able to depend on God when everything else in his life was shaken. God was constant, steady, and never changing when everything else wasn't.

Mama's Time-Out

- On a scale of 1 to 10 what is your need for consistency? Why? Have you ever considered that God is ever constant and will be the same today as He was yesterday and will be tomorrow? Let this thought sink in and anchor your heart to Him.

- Demonstrate in some way to your kids how they can count on God today. Take them to see the mountains or view some photos on the web. Ask your kids what is unique and consistent about them. Then tell them what God is like. Even though everything in life seems to change, God is constant.

Today's Love Note

Shout for joy to the LORD, *all the earth.*
Worship the LORD *with gladness; come before him with joyful songs.*
Know that the LORD *is God. It is he who made us, and we are his;*
we are his people, the sheep of his pasture.
Enter his gates with thanksgiving and his courts with praise;
give thanks to him and praise his name.
For the LORD *is good and his love endures forever; his faithfulness*
continues through all generations.

Psalm 100:1-5

I Call Him By Name

El Olam, how is it that You knew that as a mere human being I would need someone steady, something constant? As a woman and a mom, I know how quickly things change; I know how the seasons pass. Lord, my Everlasting One, thank You that when this world seems to spin out of control, all I have to do is keep my eyes on You and my heart open to You. In Your name I pray. Amen.

He's Not Finished with You Yet

There's an old saying that if you want to make God laugh, tell Him your plans. Nothing in the universe is as solid as God's plans for us, no matter what decisions we make and whether or not we think they are set in stone.

For many of us, there is one pivotal choice we made that affected the outcome of the rest of our lives. We are filled with regret and hopelessness. We see our future in terms of being over before it ever began. We lay in bed with "what if?" thoughts and daydreams.

At the awkward age of seventeen, I faced these questions. My future looked bleak. I could barely hold my head up as I walked the halls of my high school trying to ignore the stares and whispers. Even though my belly didn't yet look round, in a town of less than three thousand, there were no secrets. My secret of the baby girl growing inside me seemingly had ended my future. I remember sending up prayers to a silent God. "If you're real, You won't let this happen. If you really loved me, You'd get me out of this!"

I had a future pregnant with possibilities (no pun intended). I had dreams of going to college and starting a successful career. I never even thought of motherhood. Instead, I became a teenage mom. It was game over.

Even though motherhood came calling for me early, God's hand was in it.

Though He didn't prevent the natural consequences of sex outside of marriage, He did have plans for me as He promised in Jeremiah 29:11. "'For I know the plans I have for you,' declares the LORD, 'plans to prosper you and not to harm you, plans to give you hope and a future.'"

How could God use a mistake like this? How could this life-altering decision filled with regret give me hope and a future? These were the questions I wanted answered so badly. Instead, I watched His plans unfold over time and became amazed. Our Eternal God can take the choices we make that resulted in hopelessness and regret and shape them for His plans. He can take a choice that has life-lasting effects and turn it into something good. Nothing can outlast our God, not even the choices we make.

It was ten years later before I ever understood God's plans as He held me in His hands and guided my way. He's now using my compassion and empathy to encourage other teenage mamas that if they look to Him, He will guide them. I'm elated to share with my teen moms and their mothers that God has a plan. Every Tuesday, I smile at the new and old faces that walk through our doors for our Teen MOPS meetings. The girls come in with their babies and backpacks in tow, shouldering the burden of their choices. When they leave, they are smiling and filled with hope that they can do this "mom thing." Each mom leaves in awe of a God who cares for them and their future despite the mistakes they have made in the past.

No matter the choices we make, His faithfulness and love endure forever. He takes our weaknesses and our regrets and turns them into our strengths. The choice is ours to realize that God is eternal and we are not. Our lives are short, but we can still live them to the fullest without regret. His love for us stands the test of time, no matter what we've done.

A close friend of mine was ready to throw her life away. She thought her life was over because she couldn't live anymore with the regret and pain of the decision she made to abort her first child. Several years later God is using her decision in an unexpected manner. She is now a voice to women who find themselves in similar circumstances. After surrendering her life, her hope was ignited as God healed her regrets. Today those past regrets are seeds of hope for women hurting from their choice to have an abortion.

I can't imagine the choices you've made that cause you to shoulder your burden of guilt.

Nonetheless, they weigh you down. You aren't sure how God can use the choices you've made, but I'm asking you to turn to Him. God is ready to help you live your life to the fullest and to use your regrets for His good. No matter where you are in life and how messy you've made it, He's there—ready and waiting. He's not finished with you yet. His promise in one of my favorite Scriptures is intended for you. "But the plans of the Lord stand firm forever, the purposes of his heart through all generations" (Psalm 33:11).

Mama's Time-Out

- Make a list of your regrets. Why are they on your list? Can you see any good in them? I want to encourage you to leave your regrets on His altar and thank Him that He isn't finished with you yet. Ask Him to heal your heart of your regrets.

- Sometimes the things in life that you end up regretting are the very things you can serve God with. Take your list of regrets, and begin by accepting things as the way they are. Then ask God how He can use your regret. Is it mentoring a pregnant teen or starting a support group for women grieving over an abortion or divorce?

Today's Love Note

Your kingdom is an everlasting kingdom,
and your dominion endures through all generations.
The Lord is trustworthy in all he promises
and faithful in all he does.
The Lord upholds all who fall
and lifts up all who are bowed down.

Psalm 145:13-14

I Call Him By Name

Thank You, El Olam, for taking my burdens and my regrets and wiping the slate clean. Thank You for rescuing me from the land of regret and reminding me that no matter what I've done, Your love for me still stands the test of time and You have great plans for me. Help me to remember each time I get on my knees that You are everlasting. El Olam, this world wants me to think that my past defines my future and that I cannot rise above it. You, however, have taught me that my past can be the great blessing to my future. I'm thankful that You aren't finished with me yet. Amen.

YAHWEH ROI

The Lord Is My Shepherd

Isaiah 40:11; Psalm 23; Micah 5:4; Matthew 2:6; Revelation 7:17

*"I am the good shepherd;
I know my sheep and my sheep know me—
just as the Father knows me and I know the Father—
and I lay down my life for the sheep.
I have other sheep that are not of this sheep pen.
I must bring them also.
They too will listen to my voice,
and there shall be one flock and one shepherd."*

JOHN 10:14-16

Sheep . . . Really?

Sheep really are the most tenacious, foolish, and fearful creatures on this planet and yet God compares us to these lovely, wooly fluff balls of stubbornness. While that may be insulting and perplexing, it's true. Left to our own nature, we are like sheep, wandering mindlessly into one predicament or another.

I never really understood the parallel between sheep and my life until I was shepherding more than my fair share of kids. During a season when our budget was strapped, to make ends meet I worked at a daycare. In the mornings I cared for twelve infants, and in the afternoons I took over a classroom of three-year-olds.

The babies were my favorite. They smiled and were comforted by our familiar faces and routine. The afternoons were a different story. Being in charge of twenty three-year-olds was like herding a bunch of sheep. When one child would clobber another with a toy, others would follow suit. Like sheep, they were foolish, slow to learn, stubborn, and always demanding.

Some afternoons I prayed that we would win the lottery so I wouldn't have to come back to work. One quiet afternoon turned into a riot. A particularly obstinate kiddo was restless during naptime, stealing a blanket off of a neighboring child on her cot. Then he smacked another child in the face, causing all of them to begin crying. As I tried to police the naughty youngsters while soothing the emotional ones, the realization that something needed to change and soon weighed heavy on my thoughts in between barking commands to lay still and be quiet. They needed to listen to my voice; I needed to create structure and boundaries.

Within a week, I came to work armed with stickers, prizes, sweets, and a plan. Sitting the kids in a circle and encouraging the quiet ones with sweets, we created classroom rules. Instead of yelling to get their attention, I would whisper. When I needed them to follow me to the bathrooms, the rule was to hold hands. Soon the afternoons flew by in organized chaos. Much to my surprise, my little ones learned to listen for my voice in anticipation of prizes and praises. Soon I could herd my kids all over the church building without worrying that one would stray and without battling stubborn wills.

It was amazing to see the change in their demeanor when I arrived in their class. Other teachers took note and commented on my ability to herd twenty three-year-olds with simple commands and their willingness to follow. Like sheep listening for the voice of their shepherd, my kids were doing the same!

As the months working at the daycare flew by, I often brought in a book or two to read during naptime. I loved Sharon Niedzinski's adventures in *Heaven Has Blue Carpet* and nearly woke my kids with giggles as I read how she compared sheep and human beings. During her sixteen-year experiment of shepherding sheep and raising six kids, this suburban housewife became intimately aware of the word pictures peppered throughout the pages of the Bible where we read about God as a shepherd and people as His flock. Her practical view of seeing ourselves in these skittish balls of wool deepened my understanding of Scripture.

God's name of Yahweh Roi was more intimately understood when shepherding was the main occupation thousands of years ago. In ancient days the Hebrews were a nomadic people constantly in search of pastures for their animals. It was crucial for shepherds to keep their sheep and goats from going astray, to guard them from predators and thieves, and to supply good grazing pastures to nourish and multiply their flock. Their family's means of support literally depended on their sheep.

The first reference of God as a shepherd was by Jacob in Genesis 48:15 and later in Genesis 49:24 where he referred to God as "the Shepherd, the Rock of Israel." A shepherd is defined as someone who tends to a flock or companion. David illustrated this metaphor in Psalm 23. He described God as his own personal Shepherd, meaning he had a close relationship with God. When David penned Psalm 23, he described God's nature to provide, lead, guide, protect, save, bless, and give eternal life (Larry Richards, *Every Name of God in the Bible*).

Maybe that's why God calls Himself and His Son, Jesus, the Good Shepherd.

If we didn't have a personal Shepherd, it's likely we would succumb to our own worldly desires. Like my classroom experiment of whispering to my kiddos, it's critical to train our ears to know His voice and to guard His love within our hearts.

I've learned more than my fair share of lessons through my fierce independence. I tend to think I can do life without God there to guide me. More often than not, I fall on my rear and fail to do what I had thought I could do by myself.

Pastor Mike told me a story of a little boy who wanted to help his daddy move furniture. Dad didn't think his four-year-old little boy could do very much, so he set to work to move a desk and his son followed suit. The child planted his feet firmly on the floor and pushed his shoulder into the desk. He pushed with all his might, while his dad was really doing all the work. After grunting, shoving, and pushing for several seconds, the little boy looked up and told his daddy, "Move! You're in the way; I can do this." His father chuckled to himself and stood back to watch his son work.

How often are we like that little boy, trying to push our problem to where we want it? When we face life, we think we can do it on our own and we don't need God to be there assisting us. But when we relent and ask God for help, He leads us through our struggle. He provides all we need to face life in His pasture. But when we choose not to follow God, we become vulnerable to a world of trouble. He wants us to know Him so intimately that we can hear His voice above all others.

As Yahweh Roi looks over His flock, He is aware of our weaknesses and strengths. He is there to watch over us. Even when we choose to be stubborn and wander off, He leaves the flock to find us. He is there to nourish us with His Word and to lead us on the path of righteousness.

When you call on Yahweh Roi, you are calling on the One who watches you by night and by day. You are calling on the One who knows your needs and is ready to guide you throughout your day. You are calling on the Shepherd who sent His only Son to come and find you when you strayed from the flock. He sent His Son to lay His life down for you. He is waiting to gather you into His arms and to gently lead you.

Mama's Time-Out

 As mothers we have a tough job of tending to our little lambs. The trials and tantrums cause us to grow weary. In those moments stop and listen for His voice.

- If you want to know God more intimately as your Shepherd and better understand what Jesus taught about sheep, research the lives of sheep and shepherding, compare it to the Scriptures in the Bible.
- Here are two books I highly recommend you pick up. They will add depth to your understanding of the Scriptures, change your perspective of parenting your flock, and create a closer bond between you and the Good Shepherd: *Heaven Has Blue Carpet* by Sharon Niedzinski (Nashville: Thomas Nelson, 2008); *Scouting the Divine* by Margaret Feinburg (Grand Rapids: Zondervan, 2009).

Today's Love Note

The LORD is my shepherd, I lack nothing.
He makes me lie down in green pastures, he leads me beside quiet waters, he refreshes my soul. He guides me along the right paths for his name's sake.

Psalm 23:1-3

I Call Him By Name

Yahweh Roi, thank You for Your wisdom and Your ways. I'm ever so grateful to be part of Your flock. Lord, help me to be still so I can hear Your voice above all others. Guide my feet and lead me through life. You provide peace, safety, and comfort; and You know all my needs before I do. Help me come to know You as the faithful Shepherd who watches over my life and values me. Yahweh Roi, open my ears to Your voice so that I can hear it when trouble comes my way. Help me to hear Your call when life is blissful too, so that I can share my joys with You. In Your name I pray. Amen.

I Can Barely Shepherd My Own Sheep!

Children really should come with manuals, but then again that would be something else we would have to push out during childbirth. Babies are so tiny and helpless. At first we aren't sure what to do when they cry or how to pick them up, change them, or bathe them. (That may not have been the case for you, but I know several mamas who were intimidated with the task.) But something happens as we look into their little eyes during our first moments of awkwardness as a mom. We fall in love.

Despite our shortcomings, a bond between mother and child forms. It's so strong a mother can pick out her child's cries above all others in the nursery. We intuitively know what our child needs. The more we tend to our precious bundles, the more they begin to flourish in our care. We become their sole focus, their whole world. Soon they recognize our voice over any other mama, too.

This picture of bonding with your precious babes is the same with God. He can pick out your voice above the crowd and knows what is troubling your heart. Have you ever thought of God in that perspective? I wish I had known Him sooner. Maybe then I wouldn't have been so O.C.D. over child safety gadgets and the right way to swaddle my kids. I probably wouldn't have been so anxious either.

My parenting has been a combination of science experiments and prayers.

Coming from a dysfunctional family, I didn't have an accurate perspective of Biblical parenting. Instead, it was like the blind leading the blind. It wasn't until eight years into my experience as a mother that I began to heed the Shepherd's voice.

At the time, Cheyenne was entering into second grade. Our curlicued, hazel-eyed angel turned into a sassy, disrespectful mess. I wasn't sure how to approach her sassiness. I tried sticker charts, encouragement, and consequences with no success. It wasn't until I learned she was getting picked on that I understood the situation.

Because she had to wear an eye patch on her strong eye to help strengthen her weak eye, Cheyenne became the center of teasing and mean words. One certain girl seemed to be the ringleader. She would tease Chy unmercifully on the playground and then send her notes in class telling Cheyenne she could not be her friend. Then, the next day, she would be kind to Chy and send her notes about how she loved her and wanted to be friends. Each week it was the same, and each week my little girl was a roller coaster of emotions. Cheyenne was acting out at home because she felt safe and could let her guard down about her feelings.

When Chy finally came to me about the teasing, I realized her sassy and disrespectful behavior was her way of asking for help. She didn't need encouragement to behave or discipline to curb her sassiness; she needed me to teach her how to defend herself. As much as I wanted to tell her it was okay to smack this other child, I bit my tongue.

My husband and I talked and prayed with Cheyenne about the group of girls and the ringleader. We guided her in how to react and defend herself with prayer and kind words. Through our life experiences, we taught Cheyenne that God is with her and loves her. She learned that not everyone has Jesus in their hearts, and sometimes those without Jesus are mean. They're mean because they haven't experienced what it's like to be loved the way we are in God's hands.

We prayed for a sweet-spirited girl to be her best friend. We did as much as we could to soften the blow of getting picked on and feeling left out. The teasing stopped, but God did not send her a best friend. I had done all I could, but I still felt like I hadn't done my best. I felt I had missed something.

As I grumbled to myself about how hard it is to parent in this fallen world, His voice directed me to the only manual for kids. Any guesses? No, it wasn't some Dr. Spock book; it was the Bible. Yahweh Roi teaches us that He is the Good Shepherd. He wants us to know His voice intimately. He wants us to be able to hear Him above the static of our noisy lives. In order to shepherd Cheyenne in what is right, I too need to listen to the voice of my Shepherd.

With literally thousands of parenting books to choose from, our main objective can get lost in the topics. Should we spank or not spank, use natural consequences or a reward system? Is it better to be an authoritative parent than a permissive parent? All these books tell us that if we follow these steps, we will raise happy, well-adjusted kids. But therein lies the problem because nowhere in the Bible does God tell us to raise happy children. Instead, we are to raise obedient children. It's a radical perspective compared to the ever popular theme of raising a happy, well-adjusted child. By raising a child to be obedient, we are raising that child to be happy and well-adjusted.

The culture we live in today gives children no real limits or character. This has created self-centered children who are never satisfied and are enslaved to needing instant gratification. I have seen firsthand the effects of raising children this way. They had happy childhoods, but their adult lives are a mess. It's my desire to raise children who may be unhappy sometimes in terms of boundaries, limits, and discipline, but who are passionate for God. It's my dream to see them serve God when they become adults.

The parenting years can be rocky given the nature and personality of your child, leaving you to question if God can help you shepherd your feisty lamb. Little mama, I want to encourage you to open your Bible. You'll find God provides every example you need. If you're wondering whether to discipline or not, go to Proverbs 13:24; 19:18; or 23:13. If you need guidance on strong-willed children, check out Psalm 119:11.

As a person, I am not perfect. As a mother, I feel like I fail on a daily basis. Each day is trial and error and I wonder why God gave me a flock of kiddos, especially when I feel like I can barely hear His voice above the chaos. Through His parables and stories of being my Shepherd, His words describe grace for my errors and peace for my heart. The blessings of relying on Him to help me herd my lambs are countless. And even when I fail, I know that He still loves me and is waiting to pick me up, dust me off, and set me back in the right pasture of His grace. In turn, my kids learn by my example of going to God with my failures, my needs, and most importantly, my heart.

So far, they've learned He provides what we need. He leads us to rest at nap time. He teaches us to quiet our souls so we can hear His voice. I show my children that God's rod and staff are a comfort and so are the rules that I expect them to follow. The goal of shepherding my sheep is that they will know and love His voice. By my love for Jesus, the example I hope to show them is the passion and flame He's ignited in my heart.

Mama's Time-Out

- If possible, take your kids to a sheep farm. Observe how the sheep respond to their caretaker and refer to the references of The Good Shepherd throughout the Bible with Scriptures like Psalm 23 and John 10:14-17.

- Keep a prayer journal. You and your children can write prayers in a journal each night before bed. Be sure to record the date and leave space below the entry. Periodically go back and review your entries and see how God has answered them. In return we will be quickening our response to hear His voice.

Today's Love Note

He tends his flock like a shepherd:
He gathers the lambs in his arms
and carries them close to his heart;
he gently leads those [mamas] that have young.

Isaiah 40:11

I Call Him By Name

Yahweh Roi thank You for the manual You have set before me. It nourishes my soul and provides a path for my children to follow. Teach me to hear and follow Your voice. Let my example be a shining model for my kids. Help me show them how awesome it is to love You. Help me guide the lambs You've given me. Please provide the light and strength I need to follow You daily. Thank You for being my shepherd; thank You for Your voice. Amen.

ESH OKLAH & EL KANNA

God Is a Jealous God; God Is a Consuming Fire

Exodus 20:5; 34:14; Deuteronomy 4:23-24; Joshua 24:19; Hebrews 12:24-29

Therefore, since we are receiving a kingdom that cannot be shaken, let us be thankful, and so worship God acceptably with reverence and awe, for our "God is a consuming fire."

Hebrews 12:28-29

Striking a Balance

My son has taught me more than my fair share of lessons within the first few years of his life. Here are a few things I've learned:

- Blue sparkle toothpaste stains—*everything*.
- Glass casserole dishes make great sleds down the stairs.
- Bathtub farts are the bomb.
- Red barn paint makes great lubrication down a slide.
- Ink is an important accessory for our couch. (Applying hairspray removes it.)
- Peeing on the furniture is a means of marking territory.
- It takes 5.2 seconds to drown a fifteen-pound tomcat.
- It only takes five minutes to flood the bathroom.
- Stitches require the restraint of three nurses, a sheet, mom, and a doctor wearing a shield.
- Boys with stitches are cool.
- Powdered sugar and ceiling fans do not mix, and they cause massive amounts of vomit.
- Fish can survive in a cloud of fish food.
- Fifty-gallon fish tanks can crack in less than thirty seconds.
- The dog looks good in pink or purple paint.
- Mint green nail polish looks good on a boy but not on white carpet.

- Jumping off tables creates panic in the teachers at Sunday School.
- He can unlock all four locks on our front door in less than eighteen seconds.
- His meltdowns in public make me look evil.
- Sharing can and does induce bodily harm.
- Pushing mom's buttons is a form of entertainment.
- He really can drive his John Deere truck down the street.
- Mud and dirt make a boy feel important.
- Boys do not have mute buttons or volume control.
- Class clowns are not favored by teachers.
- Diarrhea is grounds for self-entertainment.
- Impulse control is gained over time.
- Fans, little boys, and loft beds are not a good combination.
- Peeing off the front porch is a rite of passage.
- Pestering, torturing, and terrorizing his sisters is in his DNA.
- His tender heart is protected by means of pummeling unkind friends.
- The term mom invokes images of no fun while the term dad invokes adventures.

Now that he is five, Elijah has mellowed out for the most part, although he has already set the record number of time-outs his preschool teacher has ever given—and it's only the first semester. He loves life, loves to discover, and loves experimenting. He feels very deeply and wears his emotions on his shirt. In short, his zest for life (or troublemaking) embodies the word passion. No matter the situation, he wants the full effect, good or bad. If I'm not around to steer his decision-making process (or lack thereof), his choices tend to consume him. Daily I need to enforce boundaries to teach him to win control of his flesh, temper, or emotions. Needless to say, he is a gold mine for writing material or anti-anxiety medication, take your pick. Most of my friends stalk my Facebook statuses because they love to laugh over the latest stunt Elijah pulled.

One afternoon, I watched as he became oblivious to the world as he peered into his new kaleidoscope. He was fascinated with the different shapes, colors, and reflections in his new toy. The more he rolled the end, the more intense his gaze became. No matter how I tried to rouse him, his gaze was lost in that little tube. It consumed him.

We are all like that. Someone or something catches our attention and dominates our thoughts, feelings, and actions. Our desire to know more consumes us, almost like when we experience chemistry with the opposite sex for the first time. I remember the name of the first boy I kissed. His name was Aaron, and he was one of the cool kids in seventh grade. The first few weeks I dated Aaron were wistful. I remember writing his name on my binder, books, papers, and even rigging the game m.a.s.h.

Do you remember that game? M.a.s.h. stood for mansion, apartment, shack, and home which was written at the top of a square. On either side of the square, I would then pick out four boys' names (Aaron's included) and four cars. The bottom of the square was filled with the number of kids I wanted to have. Then I'd pick a number and start counting in a circle, crossing off the name, number, house or car I landed on until all that was left was one in each category. I was thrilled when my results were Aaron, with a mansion, Mercedes, and no kids.

Much like our first kiss, we relish the moment, replaying it repeatedly in our minds. Before we know it, we have our house and number of children and their names picked out. Why, might you ask? Because we are hardwired from the day we are born to respond to what is in front of us. If we aren't careful to strike a balance, it can wreak havoc on our lives. (My obsession with Aaron brought me to a whole new level of being grounded for poor grades.)

God knew this. It's how we were created, but with Him, we can achieve balance. It's why He created boundaries and set laws in stone. He watched His children in the bonds of slavery for hundreds of years before having a chat with Moses on the mountain to work out a few minor details. Much like our toddlers, the Hebrews needed guidelines and rules lest chaos would break out because some dude lusted and committed adultery with another woman.

Rules, guidelines, and boundaries weren't meant to impose harsh restrictions and make us feel bad. They were meant to help us strike a balance and stand on solid ground.

For many years God watched His people worship idols. It caused Him to fume with anger—a righteous anger because we were destroying the good He created within us.

As the one and true living God, He created us in part to worship Him. If this wasn't established, we would find something else that catches our attention. Like my son, it would then consume us as we idolize it.

God often reveals Himself in the Bible as fire because of His jealousy for our hearts and His hatred of sin. He loves us, not the sin. Hebrews 12:28-29 sums it up: "Therefore, since we are receiving a kingdom that cannot be shaken, let us be thankful, and so worship God acceptably with reverence and awe, for our 'God is a consuming fire.'" Just like my son and many other toddlers I know, it's very easy to forget His love for us when we let other things consume our time and attention. We become mesmerized by the newest, latest, and greatest toy. As we continue to engage ourselves with our new toy, it takes God's place. Watch five minutes of TV and you'll know what I'm talking about. The world idolizes things—stuff that is not of our Father God. Ultimately, this world will fall away and God, with His precious Son, Jesus, will destroy all that opposes their holiness. Whatever we have allowed to consume our lives in place of our mighty God will be tested in fire. It will be burnt up in the flames leaving only what is good and holy. All that we have done, all that we've poured talents and dreams into, will be brought before God and tested in the flames.

Our job as mothers is to teach our children what to be passionate about with boundaries and life lessons. My prayer is that the day I stand before Jesus and He puts my life into the flames to be tested, that my efforts in raising godly children and in becoming like Christ will remain. It's also my prayer that my children's lives will be refined. I want my children to be consumed with their love for Jesus. Each day is an opportunity to fan the flames to build up what is good within us and our children.

Whether or not you have a wild stallion on your hands or a Dennis the Menace like my son, brace yourselves now for the stand-offs, the "How come I can't do that?" questions, and the constant toe stubbing of boundary lines. Now that Elijah is no longer interested in just viewing his kaleidoscope, he's been placed in time-out for experimenting the cause and effect of smacking his little sister in her face with his toy. How's that for passion?

Mama's Time-Out

 Are you aware of things that consume your attention and time? Ask God to reveal these things to you and break the habits. Is it Facebook, computer games, TV shows, unhealthy friendships, or putting activities and other commitments before God and your family?

Today's Love Note

Place me like a seal over your heart,
like a seal on your arm;
for love is as strong as death,
its jealousy unyielding as the grave.
It burns like a blazing fire,
like a mighty flame.
Many waters cannot quench love;
rivers cannot sweep it away.
If one were to give all the wealth of one's house for love,
it would be utterly scorned.

Song of Songs 8:6-7

I Call Him By Name

Esh Oklah, my heart fills with joy knowing that You love me so passionately. Set me as a seal over Your heart and carry me on the days that I can barely carry myself. Thank You that You care so much for me and that You are a passionate God, a consuming fire. El Kanna, I ask You to reveal Yourself to me in all that's around me. It fills me with awe to know You love me fiercely. Thank You for Your love and mercy. Amen.

American Idol

MOM! Why can't we get Miley's new CD? You let me listen to all her other stuff, why not now?" A young girl whined at her mom, all the while stamping her feet.

"Because I said so. Her songs aren't really for young girls anymore," her mother replied while prodding her daughter along. As I pushed my cart farther down the aisle, I glanced over at them. The daughter looked as if she was going to hyperventilate at her mother's remarks and go into shock because the CD was still sitting on the shelf and not in her hands where it ought to be. Oh, did I mention that the daughter was dressed head to toe in Miley's double identity as a singer and normal school girl . . . a.k.a. Hannah Montana? Most girls ages three to twelve have been fans of the hit Disney show *Hannah Montana* until Miley turned eighteen and opted to appeal to older audiences in her singing career.

Apparently, she idolized her. And now mom was telling her she could not worship this comedy persona anymore. Miley had recently made a career change to become more of a sensual idol versus a good, clean fun kid. It hit me then, regardless of how old we are or where we are on our path in life, what we idolize is pretty obvious to others.

As I meandered through the wonderful world of Walmart, my thoughts returned to my daily devotional time. For the last few weeks I had been reading through the Old Testament and trying to stay awake and interested in the "So and So begat So and So" when the message intertwined in these lists of names was how

God hates idols. God hates those who *worship* idols even more. It was a pattern that I noticed as I read about the rise and fall of several kings and the fall of great nations. After all it is one of the Ten Commandments. Do not worship idols.

Idols in this day and age aren't as flagrant and obvious as in the Old Testament when some carpenter or blacksmith created idols out of wood or precious metals and sold them to make a living. Let's not mention the stories of kings who even sacrificed their own offspring to the fires of Baal, or threw three young men into a fiery furnace because they refused to bow down to some huge statue. (Check the book of Daniel out for a good read.)

These days it's a bit more covert but it will suck you in faster than you can blink. It's all around us. Our nation idolizes sensuality and youthfulness. It's no wonder that the woman in front of me was buying rice cakes and nonfat food items along with a couple of magazines with the titles "How to Look Thinner in Ten Minutes," "The Five Best Tips to Improve Youthful Appearance," and my favorite, "Fifty of the Best Lovemaking Positions to Keep Your Man."

She was *maybe* a size two. My thigh is the size of her waist. While there is nothing wrong with being healthy, maintaining a balance between health and idolizing youth and thinness can be tricky if we aren't centering ourselves on God as we go about our day. If it gets out of check, we unknowingly are kneeling at the altars of beauty and youth.

Besides beauty and youth, women worry about materialism and status. Subconsciously we size up other women within view. If that woman has a better body, nicer Suburban, and is the president of the P.T.A., we tend to view her as a threat rather than befriend her. These idols also go hand in hand with malice and pride which some of us sacrifice to daily instead of being secure in who we are as an heir to God's kingdom.

This mama came to the conclusion a long time ago that beauty is fleeting. There always will be someone skinnier than me, and there always will be plenty of women who are more financially blessed than me.

It's clear to me why God commanded that we do not worship any idol. It leads us astray and makes us vulnerable to the ploy of our enemy. Besides that, God wants our total devotion. He doesn't want our divided attention. He's the kind of guy who doesn't want to share us with others. His love and devotion to us is so fierce that the jealousy and fire He feels can be compared to how we would feel if our husband cheated on us.

As a mom raising the next generation, I'm learning to open my children's eyes to the dangers of idols. "How do you do this?" you might be thinking.

My daughter's teacher taught me how during a week-long experiment over idols. She asked her students to record what they did every minute of the day including showering, reading, playing, etc. At the end of the week, she helped the students categorize their activities. It opened their eyes that most of their time had been spent on something other than focusing on God. The students were very surprised what surfaced in their lives as idols. My daughter, Cheyenne, realized that she watched TV more than she read her Bible. She made a choice to limit her TV time with help from mom, of course. I'm proud to say that she also reads her Bible before turning on the tube!

I'd much rather make a conscious choice to center myself on God rather than face His consuming fire at the end of this life. He will ultimately destroy everything that opposes or takes the place of Him. The reality is there are many idols out there and they are so easy to fall prey to. We tend to idolize what we spend the most time on or focus on. Take a moment today to ask God what has taken His place in your life. Then ask Him to ignite a fire—a passion in your heart for Him like He has for you.

Mama's Time-Out

Instructions for Idol Evaluation:
1. On a sheet of paper, record what you do daily for one week.
2. At the end of the week, categorize what you spent your time on.
3. Ask yourself and your children what things take up the most time and whether or not they have become idols.

Today's Love Note

But who can endure the day of his coming? Who can stand when he appears? For he will be like a refiner's fire or a launderer's soap. He will sit as a refiner and purifier of silver; he will purify the Levites and refine them like gold and silver.

Malachi 3:2-3

I Call Him By Name

El Kanna, Your laws and Your ways are higher than mine. I see the wisdom in Your words and commandments. Today as I pray, I ask that You refine me like gold. Test my heart, Lord, and show me what has taken Your place. Open my eyes to the potential idols that surround me and my children and ignite a passion in my heart for You. Amen.

YAHWEH

Lord

Exodus 3:1–4:31; Psalm 103:1-13; 2 Corinthians 3:7-18

"This is my name forever, the name you shall call me from generation to generation."

Exodus 3:15

Yahweh Spells What?

We spend hours and hours poring over books of names to bestow on our unborn. We research the meaning, test it out on our tongues, and daydream about the significance it will have to our child. If you're anything like me, you also take this one step further. Every name I considered was tested in the area of how other children could make fun of that name. Seriously, the very idea of naming my child a name which has the potential for getting picked on falls into the realm of stupidity.

The kids showed no mercy to me when I was in school. I was stick thin and gangly in grade school, not to mention I was practically the only white kid growing up in a heavy Mexican population. While I loved the culture, I didn't relish being teased. "Heather, the Albino Reindeer" or "Heather Whitey Feather" were names I endured.

Being scarred for life, I practiced possible names for my children and tested them every way I could possibly think of. For example, we considered naming Tori, our youngest, Alexandria. While I loved the name, I didn't like the tomboy implications or the fact that due to all the syllables it would be shortened to Lexi. Invariably she'd end up being teased as "sexy Lexi." Of course, Victoria also had its drawbacks. I knew that one day she could possibly be slammed as "not having very many secrets." However, when you feel God pressing you to name your child something, it's very hard to argue.

Then there is Elijah. I wanted something like Ethan, but like I said, when

God literally interrupts your prayer time and says, "You shall call him Elijah," can you really argue with that? As for my oldest, I thought Cheyenne was the most gorgeous name I had ever heard. I knew it was the name of a Native American tribe, but I didn't bother researching what Cheyenne really meant. You can imagine my surprise when I learned that it meant "rabbit people." Go figure…it's still a beautiful name. Later I learned that the spiritual connotation of Cheyenne means "creative." By golly, she embodies that. Our little artist is creative with color, charcoal, chalk, molding clay, and more.

There is a certain amount of destiny, traits, and character that are bestowed onto your child with the name you lovingly choose. Knowing that it is sometimes harder for boys in walk in their faith, I wanted my son to have a reminder of who he truly is and who God is. I was astounded to learn that Elijah means "Yahweh is God" and "spiritual champion." No matter what path in life Elijah chooses, he will forever remember God is God above all. He will succeed in what he does if he puts God first.

God's name, Yahweh, carries a heavy depth of meaning. It is the most intimate, proper, and precious name God has. As a matter of fact, it was so precious that Jews would substitute the name Adonay whenever they came across Yahweh. It is known as *kethive kere* which means written one way, to be read another. Yahweh occurs more than five thousand times in just the Old Testament and is the most personal name of God (Larry Richards, *Encyclopedia of Bible Words*).

The first time God revealed His name was when he was chatting with Moses about taking His people out of slavery. When God revealed His name, it was a way to reveal His heart for His people and to show that He is always present and always will be. His name also reveals His power.

So what is so significant about this name in the realm of motherhood? It is the name we are to teach our children. It shows them the need for reverence, respect, and awe. When God first spoke to Moses He said, "I AM WHO I AM." (Review Exodus 3:13-15.) Yahweh is also known as a *Tetragrammaton*, meaning it is transliterated in four-letter words that are too holy to pronounce. It's often seen as YHWH (Yahweh) or JHVH (Jehovah). It's considered His proper name. It's hard to wrap my head around. God, the only one and true living God, shared His most holy and divinely proper name with a goat herder in order to bring His people out of slavery. Can you imagine?

Listen to me, little mama. His name, Yahweh, not only indicates God's deity, it also shows His love, His mercy, and His compassion for His people. He tells Moses that it is the very reason He decided to have communication with common folk such as Moses because He heard the cries of His people coming out of Egypt and decided to do something about it.

God used these moments not only to reveal Himself to us but also to show His love for us and to get the show on the road. It was just one of His many miracles in which He revealed His power. We are to use this name in reverence and to teach our children that this is the name for the hopeless because He gives hope. It is the name for the broken because He alone can heal. It is His name for the weary because He carries us. It is the name for the hurting because He heals us. His name is true, His name is holy, and His name is worthy. His name is Yahweh.

Mama's Time-Out

- Take some time alone today and read how God delivered His children out of Egypt. Then thank Him for revealing His proper name to us. He is the kind of God who wants fellowship with us.

- Has there been a time in your life when God revealed Himself to you and, without a doubt, you knew there was a God? If not, what prevents you from seeking God as your God?

- Yahweh means "I am who I am." It describes His character. When you picked out names for your children, was it important to know the meaning of the name?

- Thank God for the name you've been given. Ask Him to speak to your heart and to help you hear Him call your name.

Today's Love Note

But I trust in you, LORD; I say, "You are my God."
My times are in your hands; deliver me from the hands of my enemies,
from those who pursue me.
Let your face shine on your servant; save me in your unfailing love.
Let me not be put to shame, LORD, for I have cried out to you; but let the wicked
be put to shame and be silent in the realm of the dead.
Let their lying lips be silenced, for with pride and contempt
they speak arrogantly against the righteous.
How abundant are the good things that you have stored up for those who fear you,
that you bestow in the sight of all, on those who take refuge in you.
In the shelter of your presence you hide them from all human intrigues; you keep
them safe in your dwelling from accusing tongues.

Psalm 31:14-20

I Call Him By Name

Yahweh, how great is Your name. Never let me be ashamed to call You my one true God. Let Your name ever be so precious to my heart. Help me to teach Your name to my children. As my Lord God, I pray that You guide this servant's heart and feet. Thank You for revealing Your name to me; it creates a kinship and opens the lines of communication. It teaches me about the depths of who You are. Direct the words on my tongue to praise Your wondrous name. Amen.

Iron Will

"Wahhhhhhhhhh. Mama, Baba!" Tori's shrills of injustice awaken me barely two hours into my sleep as I get up half naked to army crawl under her toddler bed looking for her beloved bottle. I trudge to the kitchen to refill it with water. As I tuck her back in, she glares at me while twirling her hair in one hand and thrusting the bottle in my face with the other. "Hot," she commands.

"Tori it's fine. That's all there is. Now go to sleep; its night-night time." I turn and walk away. I close her door only to hear the bottle hit the door. Rejecting the cool water, she chucks it! I ignore her screams of injustice as I crawl back into my bed.

"Hot ba-ba, no night-night!" Tori screamed for forty-five minutes. I attempted negotiations of something like, "No, Tori, your bottle is fine. Go night-night or I will take your ba-ba away." The process repeated itself until nearly 4:00 a.m. when my husband got up. Without a word to his daughter, he refilled the bottle with warm water and handed it back to her. Satisfied, Tori went back to sleep only to start the process again when her bottle was empty. Most two year olds would have caved by now or at least fallen asleep. Not my little girl. She's a freak of nature when it comes to her will.

You should have seen how determined that child was to navigate the stairs in a full leg cast. Only five minutes after returning home from the doctor's office where her leg had been put in a cast because she had fallen down the stairs, she was climbing the stairs again. Within a day she was a pro at it. Oh, did I mention—she was only ten months old?

The fact that my daughter was over two weeks late, induced twice, and weighed in at 10 lbs. 2 oz. should have clued me in to what kind of child I was giving birth to. Her iron will and larger than life personality reminds me of a wild stallion that is too spirited to be broken. Being a seasoned mom from my two previous children, I thought I had a handle on caring for an infant. Within a week of Tori's birth, I threw everything I knew out the window and chose the survival mode in order to keep from wearing a straitjacket. The girl wanted mom and only mom. She refused a binky, sippy, and bottle. Her demands were met unless I wanted to brace myself for a six-hour cry session. No joke. She wants what she wants, when she wants it, and how she wants it.

I take full responsibility for catering to her will, however, when I'm facing a day of caring for two other children on top of daycare kids and a long list of chores, I'd rather have some quiet and stability. So, at her ten-month checkup, I gave in to the doctor's prescription of weaning her in order to have my body, not to mention my life, back. After leaving for a weekend, my husband broke her of the mommy and boob pacifier only to be back to square one eleven months later.

My baby girl was in bondage to her bottle, and I was in bondage to sleep deprivation. Disciplining this girl is like getting a taste of a hell on a daily basis. Who knew that I would encounter this type of iron will as I rubbed my belly and dreamed of a sweet baby girl just a few months prior? Who knew that I would be putting this child in time-out nineteen times a day for the same offense? For those of you who understand what I'm talking about, call me. We'll start our own support group.

So how then does the Lord handle discipline like this?

Yahweh knows exactly how mothers feel. In fact, I'm going to give Him a round of applause because He had thousands of children who wandered around the desert for forty years being disciplined for many of the same offenses. They too needed a reality check. Instead of being thankful and enjoying the awesome display of His glory such as daily manna from heaven, they groaned and complained, made idols, and didn't trust Him. Did I mention they saw physical displays of His power on a daily basis?

God traveled with His people in a cloud by day and a pillar of fire by night. He gave them the commandments and set boundaries for their own good. He had a future full of milk and honey in store for them. Instead, the Hebrew slaves were much like my defiant toddler. They whined and complained. They were fussy and ungrateful, expecting the journey to be easy. Instead of being adults and appreciating the areas in their personal life that needed work, God had to discipline them for forty years. Hebrews 12:6-7 sums it up nicely: "The Lord disciplines the one he loves, and he chastens everyone he accepts as his son. Endure hardship as discipline; God is treating you as his children. For what children are not disciplined by their father?"

True love knows the value of discipline. If a child is left on her own, she will eventually turn into someone like Brett Michaels or worse yet, Marilyn Manson. A child left to his own devices is in bondage to *"It's all about me and what I want."* His spirit will suffocate at the hands of his will.

Yahweh heard His people moan and groan under the pains of slavery. After being "grounded" for four hundred years under the chains of pharaoh, God knew there was more work to be done because they had been under bondage for so long.

Being in the trenches of motherhood is much the same as leading the Hebrews around the desert for forty years. If the area of bondage isn't broken and obedience is not attained, then we need to lead our children in circles until the lesson is learned. It's not just the behavior that needs to change; it's the heart that we are after.

Discipline means high standards that Marilyn and Brett were never shown. It means learning to break the will of our child without breaking her spirit. It means teaching our children right from wrong, correcting their behavior, and explaining the reason. All this is done in a way that doesn't break the heart-to-heart connection with our child. We go from being their commander in the toddler years, to coaching them about their choices in the tween years. Then as they continue to grow, we become their counselor in the teen years and consultants when they are adults. During these stages, we give correction, guidance, consequences, and praise. We also give grace and humility in the same way Jesus does for us.

Yahweh grants humility, peace, and light to guide our willing feet and hearts. I love God with all my heart, soul, and strength. This depth of love carries over into how I correct my children. While I take responsibility for building up Tori's will during the time I played the Ultimate Survivor, it's time to break the bad habits I've allowed her to keep. Though there are days when I'm banging my head against the wall dreaming of my previous occupation as a vacation destination, I know that a few months from now she will be better off with the discipline I am giving her.

The lessons God will want to teach her will be easier lessons later on in life because she learned to obey her mother. Remember the correction process of being the commander is unpleasant now, but your child and his co-workers, friends, teachers, and in-laws will thank you later. If you feel like you are going to blow your top, send your lovely deviant to her room for a time-out and focus on what triggered your feelings of anger. Then, after counting to a million or watching at least one episode of *19 Kids and Counting,* go in for round two and three or four if necessary. Your child will eventually get the point that your will is stronger than hers. Why? Because God is with you and knows oh so well what you are going through. (Remember, He disciplined for forty years versus the few years you've been disciplining.) Go to Yahweh and pour out your frustrations. It's okay. He knows how you're feeling, and He has the tools in hand when you're ready.

Yahweh didn't come to lead His people out of slavery only to leave them in bondage. He came so we would know Him intimately and obey His voice when He calls. He calls because He loves us and wants the best for us. Yahweh wants to be known so intimately He left us a love letter full of inspiration, wisdom, and tactics. And He's given us the privilege and responsibility to pass His love letter on to the next generation.

Mama's Time-Out

- What are your discipline tactics? Do you feel they need some tweaking?
- Do you attempt to control your children and the situation or let them experience negative consequences from their choices?
- When you know you have reached your limit, take a time-out. Then evaluate the root issue. Is it because you are tired? Are the kids grouchy because they are hungry? Is your child upset because of what her sibling did?
- When time-outs for both you and your child haven't worked and you are still grouchy, go for a walk or run errands and let Daddy handle the brigade.

Today's Love Note

The LORD will establish you as his holy people,
as he promised you on oath, if you keep the commands
of the LORD your God and walk in obedience to him.
Then all the peoples on earth will see that you are
called by the name of the LORD, and they will fear you.
The LORD will grant you abundant prosperity—in the fruit of your womb,
the young of your livestock and the crops of your ground—in the
land he swore to your ancestors to give you. The LORD will
open the heavens, the storehouse of his bounty, to send
rain on your land in season and to bless all the work of your hands.
You will lend to many nations but will borrow from none.

Deuteronomy 28:9-12

I Call Him By Name

Yahweh, how gracious is Your peace, how amazing is Your authority. The cry of my heart is to bring You praise. I want my children to be fully grounded in how they are raised and established in Your name. Help me to teach them to love and respect You, Lord. Thank You for my children and their personalities. I pray that each one serves You and brings glory to Your name alone. Thank You, Yahweh, for Your Word and Your wisdom. Amen.

ADONAY

Master

Genesis 15:2; Exodus 4:1-5, 10-15; Deuteronomy 10:17; Psalm 16:2; Luke 17:13

Give thanks to the Lord of lords:
His love endures forever.

PSALM 136:3

Who's the Boss?

Between the hours of 12:00 a.m. and 11:59 p.m. I am at my family's beck and call, meaning I am on the job twenty-four hours a day, seven days a week. There have been times in my career as "Mommy" when I worked outside the home only to quit because I couldn't balance my family's needs and my boss's expectations.

Most days my living room looks like a toy store. There are over twenty loads of laundry to be washed, and I find myself gasping by 3:30 in the afternoon because I still haven't made it to the bedroom to put on decent clothes. I haven't even brushed my hair or put on a bra. (What's the point? Between gravity and breastfeeding three children, underwire is just a hassle.) In this season of motherhood, I can't even form one thought without someone screaming at me for help.

Case in point—all three kids finally got their own bedrooms. For the last eighteen months, Tori and Elijah shared a room and Cheyenne had the bedroom next to them. Because Tori doesn't require much sleep, she stirred the pot during our nighttime routine. She would even awaken her brother in the middle of the night and both would creep out of their rooms, causing mischief and mayhem. After months of not getting any sleep, my husband built a new bedroom in our basement for Cheyenne and we moved Elijah to her old room.

Within five minutes (maybe it was seconds, but I'm giving them the benefit of the doubt) of their rooms being organized and assigned, Elijah hit Tori. She came into his room and refused to leave. He clocked her with one of his big metal trucks. In retaliation, she clamped down in the middle of his back with her teeth and held on for all it was worth. Since that lovely moment, I have been in negotiations of who can play where, how, why, and when.

If they aren't fighting, then they are constantly asking when I will serve their next snack, flip the channel to the show they want, cook what they like for supper, dress them in what they want to wear, and take them on social outings. Somehow I've lost my title as Mama-Boss and have become Mama-Servant to Neanderthals who aren't even half my body weight. Do you see where I'm going with this yet?

Serving your family is one thing, but becoming a slave and meeting their every desire is another. If we aren't careful, the role we play raising our children and serving our family can and will turn us into doormats. Dear mama, listen closely. We were not put on this earth with our gifts in nurturing and high pain tolerance to become doormats. We were put here to nurture, guide, and serve our families in the way that Jesus served us in His three short years of ministry on this earth.

Serving God starts with serving our families. It is the purest form of love and shows the heart of our mighty God. He sent His Son Jesus to serve us by taking our place on the cross. In fact, once we put ourselves under His leadership, we find our true sense of purpose and our daily lives are put into perspective.

Motherhood isn't just about nurturing and doing everything for them. We know we won't always be there to help our children. One day we will launch our kiddos into the world. Since birth we have been preparing them for that day. Instead of doing everything for them, I'm learning through trials and error it's better to step back and ask, "What are *you* going to do?" This puts the problem back into their hands, keeps me from being a doormat, and teaches them to rely on their God-given abilities and strengths. Jesus did the same when He hung out with His disciples. He spoke in parables, encouraging His followers to think for themselves and to search their hearts for the right answer.

When we call on the name Adonay, we are in essence defining our relationship with God and laying down our lives to be His servants. Adonay means LORD. It appears more than three hundred times in the Hebrew Scriptures. Adonay was often used to replace Yahweh in the ancient scrolls. When Adonay and Yahweh appeared together in the Bible, it was read as "Sovereign LORD" or in other translations as "LORD God." Adonay is first found in Genesis 15:2. When we call on His name, we are aligning our hearts and homes under His leadership (Larry Richards, *Every Name of God in the Bible*).

Often, in the madness of mothering, we somehow forget the chain of command. This leadership and authority is lost in translation because our children do not see us deferring to His leadership. Maybe, we are too busy doing everything for them and haven't taught our kids the foundation of authority and leadership. We forget we are to serve God first, husbands second, and our children third. (Such a strange concept to put on paper, isn't it?)

Another case in point: My oldest daughter often arrived home from school and threw her backpack in the middle of the living room floor followed by her coat, shoes, and whatever else she needed to shed all in the name of cartoons and fun. Once I realized that my role as a mother had become invisible and that I had enslaved myself by picking up after her, I seriously considered a straitjacket. She didn't view me as her mother but as her personal maid.

As I thought about what needed to change, I wondered what had happened. How had I managed to teach Cheyenne that it was okay to treat me as a maid as she left a trail of stuff throughout the house? The same went for her room, missing papers, and schedule mishaps. Inadvertently I had taught her that I would rescue her no matter the situation, late and lost homework included. In the process, I had reduced God as some big dude in heaven who tossed out commandments and warm fuzzies. I had failed to teach her that she needed to respect Him and me.

When we bring children into this world, part of our job is to teach them to respect us. This respect applies to their parents being in authority. As they grow up, and if we have purposefully taught them what respect is, they will have learned reverence for God.

After this huge revelation, I did what any self-respecting mama would do. I "cleaned house." I lined up my troops and told them that no longer would I be taking care of them. Instead, I handed out their chore charts and house rules along with the consequences if they were not followed. I figured if I am governed by God and the choices I make, they needed to learn this truth too. I also asked for forgiveness for enabling them to treat me as a personal maid and explained the importance of respecting Mama.

My children sat on the couch with a "deer in the headlight" look. They weren't sure if I had seriously lost my mind or if I was actually sincere. Once they realized the free ride was over and they needed to be more responsible for themselves, they panicked.

Granted, in the weeks since that fateful day there have been many setbacks; however, I have already seen growth in my children. They care more about their things, their rooms, and me. I'm no longer slipping in water left on the bathroom floor. I'm de-cluttering less, and my sanity is now in a better state. (I'm not wearing a straitjacket or pulling out my hair.)

Making my children responsible for themselves leads them back to Christ and calling Him Adonay. Jesus came to this earth as a servant, but He literally drew a line in the sand. Yes, He hung out with prostitutes and greedy thieves, but He also commanded respect with His example of love, guidance, and boundaries. He used parables to gently rebuke sinners. (Review all of Matthew 13.) In these parables, God is asking that we submit ourselves to His leadership and respect Him and ourselves enough to live the life He intended.

Christ came so that we might also understand who our real masters are. Not only did Jesus come to teach us obedience, He used His Father's glory to cast out demons and calm the winds. One of my favorite examples of Jesus as Master is when He fell asleep on a boat. Terrified of the storm that suddenly came upon them, His disciples woke Him. He rebuked them for their lack of faith and then rebuked the wind and the waves. The sea immediately obeyed His command (review Mark 4:35-40).

Raising children includes teaching them to hear and obey our voice, so that they will be able to transfer this obedience to God. Even if it means taking drastic measures and cleaning house like I did, the goal isn't commanding obedience. Jesus didn't command obedience; He asked us to love Him as our Master and Lord.

What I've noticed throughout the New Testament is Jesus gave choices. He didn't give commands. With the choices, He also spoke of God's deep love. More often than not, the people He spoke to wanted to follow Him. They fell in love with Him and obedience was the result. The same goes for our kids. When we lovingly give choices, allow consequences, and gently rebuke them, they will want to do what is right because they love us. The reward is keeping our sanity and raising great kids!

Mama's Time-Out

> Have your children taken over as little masters? If so, I highly recommend a few tools to help you in that department. You don't have to follow and apply every child-rearing book you read. Raising children is a science, You read books and gain advice from friends. Then you take what you learn and apply it in a way that works for you. Here are some potential tools for you.
>
> Helpful resources for your mothering skills: *Momology: A Mom's Guide to Raising Great Kids* by Shelly Radic (Grand Rapids: Revell, 2010). Another

great resource, *What's in the Bible for Mothers* by Judy Bodmer and Larry Richards (Bloomington, MN: Bethany House, 2008). Also, *Loving Your Kids On Purpose,* by Danny Silk (Shippensburg, PA: Destiny Image Publishers, 2008).

Today's Love Note

One day Jesus said to his disciples,
"Let us go over to the other side of the lake."
So they got into a boat and set out. As they sailed, he fell asleep.
A squall came down on the lake, so that the boat was being swamped,
and they were in great danger. The disciples went and woke him,
saying, "Master, Master, we're going to drown!"
He got up and rebuked the wind and the raging waters;
the storm subsided, and all was calm.
"Where is your faith?" he asked his disciples.
In fear and amazement they asked one another, "Who is this?
He commands even the winds and the water, and they obey him."

Luke 8:22-25

I Call Him By Name

Father God, who am I that You would share Your most holy name? I am humbled at the depths of Your love for me and thank You for the tools You've laid out for me to use. Adonay, I pray that I can teach my children to obey my voice so that later they will learn to hear and obey Yours. I ask for the strength and wisdom needed to raise my children. Help me to bend their wills and not break their spirits. They are a mighty work in Your hands; help me guide them. In Your holy name, Adonay, I pray. Amen.

Masters in Disguise

Okay ladies, listen up. I've got a dirty little secret—well more like two or three. They're not pretty, and you may be disgusted with me and choose not to read any further. But for those of you who like getting the inside scoop, here it goes.

I used to have several masters, namely two. Would you like to know their names? Well, they have several brands, but they boil down to cigarettes and beer. Yes, smoking used to call my name and demand that I light up when I was stressed, upset, bored, happy, nervous, angry, etc. Alcohol was used to take the edge off, celebrate, cope with major events, and relax. I know, it sounds trashy and terrible, doesn't it? Some of you may have dropped the book already. Still others may wonder what's so bad about these two. Nothing really, unless they take center stage from God. He should be the one and only master we ever serve.

How can a gal like me who sounds so Christian have secrets like this? I come from over five generations of alcoholics and addicts. If you ever want to read the psych evaluation prepared by some shrink for my DUI hearing, let me know. You'll have a good laugh, because that is not who I am today. But please understand that drinking alcohol is pretty much a "no-no" for me now. That revelation came after my body was slammed against the back of a cop car and I was arrested. (This was back in my college days when, of course. I *knew* my rights.)

We all have coping strategies, and mine came in the form of harmful substances that helped alter my perception so I didn't have to deal with the root of my problems. After my arrest and review of all the lovely labels the shrink gave me, I knew I needed to make a decision because the masters I served were slowly poisoning me. No matter how normal my substance abuse was to my fellow college friends, deep down I knew something about the whole situation wasn't right. Despite some extremely painful consequences, I continued drinking and smoking until I heard God whisper into my decaying life, "Which master will you choose, Heather?"

"Hmmm, gee God, I don't know. I rather prefer the instant results of the substances I use. Of course, I want You, God. I just don't know how to get there!"

When God approached me about changing my habits, He opened my eyes to the deception of my masters. It was very unsettling because this was how I was wired, or so I thought. It was how I'd been taught to cope. My earliest memories of my father involved drinking and drugs. To me this was *normal*. So when it was time to align my allegiance with God and walk away from these masters, it was like asking me not to breathe ever again, to jump on a plane to Africa to help orphans, to rob a bank.... It was not normal; it was extreme.

God was asking me to make Him master over my entire life with no area off limits. He was asking me to fully rely on Him. He was asking that I turn to Him in moments of frustration and when I was overwhelmed, panicked, and stressed. He was asking me to wait for His voice and follow His commands.

Of course, this literally meant entirely rearranging how I functioned. The process was not easy at first as my flesh and stress cried louder than His voice, but as I submitted to His leadership, the process got easier. (It helped that my husband bought a forty-pound professional boxing bag, too.) The more I looked to the Master for His call on how to handle a situation, the more it became the natural and normal thing to do.

Nowadays I'm the most levelheaded and sane person in the Shaw clan. Not only do I have a clear mind and clean lungs, but I'm teaching my children to rely on God. So let me ask you a few questions:

- What Master or masters do you currently serve?
- What are the benefits and, most importantly, do your habits align with God?
- Do you hear God's voice and submit to His authority?

If you aren't sure how to answer these questions, then plant your mama butt down and ask God to reveal what master you serve. There are all sorts of masters out there, not just substances like mine. Other ones that God has helped me weed out over the years affect more than just me and my kids. At one point or another they affect everyone. Not sure what I'm talking about? Look at the list below and see which ones catch your attention.

- Selfishness
- Laziness
- Pride
- Self-pity
- Critical tongue
- Judging others
- Conceit
- Comparisons
- Bitterness
- Self-exaltation
- Materialism
- Financial status
- Emotional eating
- Not placing Christ first

This list isn't meant to offend you. It's meant to help point out where God is trying to get your attention. These characteristics and traits are sneaky; most often they are passed on to the next generation because our children learn by watching us. I can write about this because "I've been there and done that" so to speak. Believe me, I know the damage each of these masters cause as we become enslaved to them instead of serving our mighty God. It causes our spirits to harden and become calloused, making it difficult to respond to the nudging of the Holy Spirit.

This has probably been the most depressing chapter for you, so let me remind you that our Lord knows everything about us. He knows us so well and can pave the way to help us when we choose to call Him Master. When we are ready, He will help us through any issue or habit we need to break. He knows us so well because He created us. God also knows that unless we allow Him to be Adonay, we will fill the place that belongs to Him with something else.

Dear little mama, go to Him with your issues. Lord knows we all have 'em. Surrender to Him. He will have compassion on you. He will not only fix your issues, He will work with you to free you from your addictions, hang-ups, habits, and chains. He will also vindicate you (see Psalm 135:14). Your struggles and hardships will not be wasted. Your children will see your victory and help you celebrate in your journey to break free. By going through this life lesson you also will be teaching your babies that God matters. They will in turn learn to rely on Him and serve Him. So, little mama, what are you waiting for? Call Him Adonay.

Mama's Time Out

- After reading about my struggles, what do you sense God asking you to work on?
- What are your priorities? Have any of them taken God's place as the one in charge?
- When we begin to put God first in our lives, we begin to impress this importance on our children's hearts. Begin with little examples for your kids. My kids do not get to turn on the TV until they've had their Jesus time.
- Because we know our children's weaknesses, I pray for them. Elijah hates not being first in everything. I help him work on this issue of pride in small ways that apply to him before he grows up and it begins to master him. You can do the same for your own children.

Today's Love Note

*Therefore, if anyone is in Christ,
the new creation has come:
The old has gone, the new is here!*

2 Corinthians 5:17

I Call Him By Name

Adonay, You know my heart and You know what I struggle with. Sometimes it's hard to hear Your voice through my hang-ups and insecurities. As I come before You today, I ask that You cleanse my heart and help me remember that I serve You only. If there is an area in my life that I need to work on, reveal it to me, Adonay. Lord, apart from You, I have no good thing. Amen.

YAHWEH ROPHE

The Lord Who Heals

Exodus 15:26; Isaiah 30:26; Mark 2:3-12; Luke 5:17

*"This is what the L*ORD*, the God of your father David says:
I have heard your prayer and have seen your tears; I will heal you."*

2 KINGS 20:5

Speedy Recovery

Henoch-Scholein Purpura—no, the kids did not get hold of my computer. The word, my dear little mama, is a disease my daughter came down with in second grade. Three doctors and several exams could not diagnose what was making her legs break out in a bloody rash, nor could they identify the reason for the pain. We had just gotten finished going on a long walk one cool fall evening when we noticed that the top of Cheyenne's feet were dark red. Thinking she had trampled through poison ivy, we took her to the pediatrician who assumed the same thing and prescribed an anti-itch cream.

Several hours later, the rash began crawling up her legs, turning bright red and moist. Cheyenne also had intense pain, blood in her urine, and other strange symptoms. She had the not-so-fun stuff like vomiting, fever, and diarrhea. By that time it was late in the night and this mama wasn't going to stop at anything to get relief for her baby girl. After reaching the on-call doctor, I was given the runaround. She did not think Cheyenne's symptoms were related, nor did she feel the need to prescribe anything for the pain other than Tylenol®. Mama-bear objected. I wanted my daughter pain free until we were able to get in to see the doctor the next morning. By the time I finished the phone call, that doctor was pretty much in fear of her life. She said she'd rather be on the wrong side of a rifle than to have to deal with me.

The next two days Cheyenne was in so much pain that she could not even walk to use the restroom nor could she sleep. Her pain medication barely took the edge off. We were in and out of the clinic while doctors ran tests and looked up symptoms. All we could do was continue to rely on our feverish prayers that God would help the doctors diagnose the cause.

The third day of Cheyenne's mysterious illness our friend Dr. Dave (he's technically a physician's assistant, but we call him Dr. Dave because we are part of the same church family and he's been there for all the ugliest of illnesses with our kids). He called and asked us to bring Cheyenne back in to see his friend, Dr. Finkner, who specialized in skin disorders. Dr. Finkner walked in the room, and before he even introduced himself, he knew immediately by sight what was ailing our baby girl. God had led us to the right place. Dr. Finkner's daughter had fallen ill to the same disease less than a year earlier. He faxed the results to our pediatrician and together they worked out a treatment plan for Cheyenne.

HSP is a rare blood disorder in which the blood vessels become inflamed and burst which leads to bruising under the skin (a.k.a nasty rash with *immense* pain). In very few cases it can also affect the kidneys and lead to kidney failure. The illness generally lasts four to six weeks and there is no cure for it. All we could do was take her to be tested twice daily to ensure it wasn't affecting her kidneys and to treat the symptoms.

After discovering her diagnosis and knowing that it *was* affecting her kidneys, I called our church and every other possible prayer warrior with the official diagnosis and asked them to pray. I was encouraged to do so because of Matthew 18:19-20:

> *Again, truly I tell you that if two of you on earth agree about anything they ask for, it will be done for them by my Father in heaven. For where two or three gather in my name, there am I with them.*

This Scripture reveals God hears our prayers. Most often, when I've been in prayer groups, it is referenced for healing. Yahweh Rophe means the God who heals. (Keep in mind that Jesus, God, and the Holy Spirit are one and yet three separate beings. It helps to think of them as an egg. There is the shell, the egg white, and yolk—all in one frame, yet three different separate parts.)

Remember the story of the Israelites after Moses helped free them from over four hundred years of bondage? They often needed reminders that God was in control. God called Himself Yahweh Rophe as He warned the Hebrews to abide His warnings and obey His commands so He would not inflict any of the diseases on them as He had inflicted on the Egyptians.

The name *Rophe* in Hebrew means to cure, heal, make whole or to restore (Larry Richards, *Every Name of God in the Bible*). In the New Testament we again see God and Jesus working as one as our source of healing. During the days that Jesus walked the earth He healed the sick, made the lame walk, made the blind see, raised the dead to life, and healed skin diseases like leprosy. God worked through His Son, Jesus, to restore hearts and souls, cleared out demons, and brought back sanity. (Yes, girls I empathize with this because I ask Jesus to grant me sanity and serenity on a daily basis.) He is our ultimate healer.

Miracles still happen in the world today where a child is suddenly cured of leukemia or a man is healed of a terminal disease. There are other cases where God chooses to use modern-day medicine as a means to heal our illnesses. I have no qualms with it. I thanked God for the medicine used to help me through my postpartum depression. In Cheyenne's case, Yahweh Rophe sped up the healing process and I truly believe it's because we all gathered together in prayer, faithfully asking Him to heal her. Even when we are too weak to have any faith left, God provides just what we need. Remember the story of the mustard seed and Jesus? (Review Matthew 17:20.) This isn't always the case, sometimes God doesn't choose to heal us, but He does give us more faith. While we may not understand His ways when He takes a loved one home and we despair in the aftermath that we didn't pray enough. We have a choice even then to keep our faith or waver because our prayers weren't answered.

Within two weeks of coming down with HSP, Cheyenne's illness cleared up. It was if she went to bed with the flu and woke up cured the next morning. Cheyenne's test results also showed that she was completely normal. It left the doctors perplexed because the disease normally takes at least four weeks to run its course in the body. God heals. It may be something as complex as cancer to something as simple as a common cold, but He heals. He cares for us each day. He watches and protects our bodies, hearts, and minds.

So instead of turning to your vitamin C or rummaging through your medicine cabinet, *first* pray with your children. Help your child ask God for healing when she scrapes her knee or he has a tummy ache. Ask Him to take the sickness away. Not only will this build your faith, it will also be a teaching moment for your babies that God is the source of healing. It will create an impression on their hearts to turn to Him in their time of need. Even if He doesn't heal, we can still teach them to have faith.

Mama's Time-Out

What Scriptures do you rely on when your little ones are sick? Do you immediately pray for healing? Even if it's a little scratch or a bump, praise God for His mighty hands and ask Him to heal your child. My favorite Band-Aids I use for my kids are the brand, Band Angel. They have Scripture verses about God's power to heal and cute little angels. Visit http://bandangels.net/ to buy a box or two.

Today's Love Note

*Is anyone among you in trouble? Let them pray. Is anyone happy?
Let them sing songs of praise. Is anyone among you sick?
Let them call the elders of the church to pray over them and
anoint them with oil in the name of the Lord.
And the prayer offered in faith will make the sick person well;
the Lord will raise them up. If they have sinned, they will be forgiven.
Therefore confess your sins to each other and
pray for each other so that you may be healed.
The prayer of a righteous person is powerful and effective.*

James 5:13-16

I Call Him By Name

Yahweh Rophe, how precious is Your name. Your Word says that if we gather together and pray, it will be done according to Your will. Help us understand what Your will is in every situation. I pray Your words inspire me to pray for our health as well as healing my heart when needed. You don't just put salve in my wounds; instead, You heal my hurts. Your Word binds up the brokenhearted, brings health to the bones, sews up the marrow, and heals my diseases. Thank You, Lord, for Your Son, Jesus. Help me to call on Him to intercede and to touch ailing bodies. In Your precious name I pray. Amen.

Redeemed

Everyone has a past, some more colorful than others. Even my son who is almost six years of age has a past that precedes him wherever he goes. (The preschool teachers in this town were drawing straws to see which one would be "blessed" with his presence.) At times it irritates me that he is judged before they've ever met him, much less taken the time to get to know the boy.

I know he's a colorful character, but it's more about the fact that they haven't readily given him a chance. I know what it's like to have a past like that, to be judged before anyone has taken the time to get to know me. I have several labels in this town; all of which I've brought on myself, unintentionally. Before I came to Christ, I was bound in many illnesses, most of them mental. Not sure what I'm talking about little mama? Here's a good example, I spent three years away from my parents and siblings because of monstrous mistakes I had made. I was busy trying to patch it all back together. Then a couple of years later one of my little brothers came to live with us while he was getting his life back on track after getting divorced at the age of nineteen.

Because he was searching out career possibilities in law enforcement, he decided to go on what's called a "Ride Along" with the Kearney Police Department. (All police departments allow this so long as you wear a bullet-proof vest, sign your life away, and go on nights when statistically there are not many crime possibilities.) Apparently, my brother mentioned that I was his sister. The officer thought my name was familiar and decided to look up my name... bad idea. Not only did it bring up my name, but it also brought up every offense I had ever committed. That ride along was eight years ago and to this day my brother has not let me live it down, nor has the rest of my family. Make no mistake, no matter how hard you try to hide and cover your past, it WILL find you.

At first when little things like that would happen, I was able to brush it off and think "No big deal!" Then after my past sabotaged potential careers and eventually affected who my kids got to play with, I was annoyed. The last straw was when we applied for life insurance and I found that no company would touch me with a ten-foot pole. I was told they would consider me in *six to ten years* because I was too much of a risk. I was devastated, granted I was nine months pregnant with my last child at the time the rejection came. I sat there staring down at my huge belly while rubbing my swollen fingers over it wondering when all this judgment was going to end.

I wondered if any of the painful progress I had made over the years was worth it. It seemed that no matter how much I had changed, it wasn't enough, it didn't matter. After everything was said and done, I moped around the house trying to make sense of it all. Early one morning as I sat on the couch trying to catch my breath from tackling my son (he tried to chase Daddy's truck to say goodbye before Daddy left for work), I had an epiphany; funny how these happen when I'm ready to throttle my child. Elijah had just been forgiven and redeemed in my eyes for his offense, even though he knew it wasn't a good idea to get up at 7:00 a.m., unlock all three locks on the front door, run outside, and chase Daddy's truck down the street. He was desperate to say goodbye and didn't understand that his behavior was not acceptable. Elijah did understand he was forgiven through my open arms and words I spoke to him.

He was redeemed even though I knew no matter how hard he tried, he would have other faux pas moments and offend again. He wasn't redeemed because of his efforts as he tried to be good. He was redeemed because I extended grace to him. As I sat hugging my son as best as I could with my huge belly, my heart recognized that the same grace that I was giving to my son God had given to me.

God called me out of my depths of sin and redeemed me because my Jesus, my great High Priest acted on my behalf when He spilled His blood for me. Jesus stood before God and asked for pardon on my behalf. During the process of falling in love with Jesus, He healed the wounds on my heart that were inflicted during my lifestyle of sin and being genetically pre-dispositioned to mental health issues (thanks again Mom and Dad). It wasn't because of my efforts of trying to be good; it was by God's grace granted to me through Jesus that I am redeemed.

In the process of loving Jesus, He naturally restored my heart. His presence rippled into every part of my life, with peace, hope, and restoration. When God pulls us from rock bottom, after searching for us in the dirtiest and loneliest of places, He strips us of the judgments and labels we've obtained by our past and cleanses us with the blood of His Son. He takes our crimson-stained garments and dresses us in garments that are whiter than snow.

Friends and family may still be judgmental and hold us to the status quo of "But I know what she did," even after we have been transformed by God's love; but as we stand before God, He only sees the blood from His Son and knows that we are pardoned—our past forgotten. Regardless of how friends and family may judge and be critical of me or my children, God reminds me He *sees me* differently. He looks at my heart, not my past. He reminds me that it wasn't friends and family who came and rescued my heart, Jesus did. The day Christ died, He pleaded with God on my behalf and took responsibility for my sin. He atoned for my past. Your life and your name were written on Jesus' heart and hands as He hung from the cross. Regardless of how your town may talk about you, remember who it was that rescued you.

Failures, mistakes, and trials are covered under His definition of redemption. So accept the grace He's given you and do your best to love Him today. I know that I've already extended grace to my son a thousand times over. The probability of Elijah committing another offense is quite likely, so I'll continue to show God's mercy and grace to him just as God extends grace to me on a daily basis.

Stop for a moment, it's time to let go of your past. Nothing you say or do will get you into heaven's gates unless you accept that you are a redeemed child of God. No amount of trying to forgive yourself or holding yourself accountable pleases God. Instead it insults the very nature of God. It diminishes what Jesus did on your behalf. So let go and let it be. Let God call you His beloved and let the joy of redemption fill your heart.

Mama's Time-Out

 What is your definition of redeemed?

> If you haven't accepted the redemption God has provided you, journal your past and sins. Then, one by one ask for forgiveness. When you've finished, torch the paper. This symbolizes how God remembers your sin no more. This will help you see how God has forgiven you and has redeemed you.

Today's Love Note

Praise the LORD, my soul; all my inmost being, praise his holy name.
Praise the LORD, my soul, and forget not all his benefits—
who forgives all your sins and heals all your diseases,
who redeems your life from the pit and crowns you with love and compassion.

Psalm 103:1-4

I Call Him By Name

Yahweh Rophe, redemption is a wondrous thing. Sometimes, it is difficult for me to move beyond my past. I can't understand how You have separated me from my sins, as far as the East is to the West. You alone can redeem. I pray as I go about my day that Your love quiets my soul and drowns out the words of those who condemn and judge me. I call on Your mighty name to heal the wounds of the past and redeem who I am in Your eyes. I pray that Your presences dwells in my heart and redeems my soul daily. In Your wondrous name, Amen.

YAHWEH SHALOM

The Lord Is Peace

Judges 6:24; 2 Thessalonians 3:16

You will keep in perfect peace those whose minds are steadfast, because they trust in you.

Isaiah 26:3

Peace Within

While researching the name Yahweh Shalom, I asked a few Facebook Stalkers... err, friends, to tell me how God has granted them peace in their times of trouble. With permission to quote them, here is what they wrote:

> **Me:** Okay Chicas, researching how God brings us peace, any thoughts?
>
> **Marla:** While in Lincoln, with both parents in the Nebraska Heart Institute Hospital, as the Doctor and four nurses were working on my Mom, I had to leave her room while she was in real trouble. I walked over to the window and prayed. "God you know I am powerless I cannot help or save my Mom. I've brought her to the best place I know and the doctors and nurses can only do so much. She needs you to touch her. If it is in your will to take her to be with you, then I know you will help us." An entire being (spirit, soul, and body) of peace came over me.
>
> Recognizing my *powerlessness* and abandoning myself to him always brings peace. The abandoning is what I struggle with and then I wonder why I don't have peace. How that relates to being a mom... well I had to do that over and over with my children. I couldn't micro manage their lives. Even when they were young

and being taken out of my arms for surgery or when they were in the hospital and the knowledge that I couldn't "fix" them to letting them get on that bus for Kindergarten, drive a car, or date. Peace is knowing that God only loaned them to me and they really aren't mine.

Leslie: Marla's posts make me tear up. Especially her quote about her kids... "Peace is knowing that God only loaned them to me and they really aren't mine." SO TRUE! And I know that I will have to do that... countless times with my babies in the future...

Amanda: God brings me peace in His Word. Up until the last 3 years of my life, I only read and meditated on His Word when I felt like it (very infrequent). Now that God has pulled me closer to Him through His Word, I feel an overwhelming peace—especially when I am reading and studying the Bible. I also never thought memorizing verses would be useful. I was so wrong. God's peace surrounds me in sad or lonely moments as I quietly recall from memory select verses of His Word. (Hope this helps) Have fun writing! :)

Angie: Prayer. Phil 4:6-7.

I can relate to all of these posts because my heart is literally walking around in three little bodies. Plus this mama is a total control freak and feels the need to micromanage every detail of her children's lives. (I'm seriously debating on starting a control freaks anonymous. Would you come to the meetings?) Everything, from how they get dressed to dictating how their teachers may interact with them. (But I do give them as much freedom and choices as I possibly can; for example, I put the kids' clothes away in outfits, instead of pants and shirts in separate drawers!) After my son's birth I learned that I had to let go and place him and my other kids into the hands of the Father.

When Elijah was born, it was touch and go. He had a life-threatening case of jaundice and a heart murmur. To make matters even more stressful, he was not gaining weight and his doctor wanted to me to consider formula. Not that I had anything against formula, we just could not afford the extra expense. Worries and doubts filled my mind. No matter how much I tried to fight for him, I couldn't will for his body to be well or to gain weight. I couldn't will that his heart murmur heal.

Finally after discussing our options with his pediatrician, I struggled to surrender his life to the Lord. As mothers we feel it's in our power to control all that happens to our precious babies. Soon reality sets in and we learn brusquely, we cannot control the world; instead, we have to trust God. When I did, a peace that I cannot begin to describe settled over me. Gone were the doubts. Gone were the thoughts of worry. Similar to what Marla described, my body, soul, and spirit was washed in a wave of peace that I never knew existed. God provided peace for my heart and for Marla as her mother battled for her life.

Oftentimes as women of God, we ask ourselves why bad things have to happen. We ask where God is in the midst of it. We question if we could have prevented it. We sometimes think, because we are children of God, that no harm or mayhem should come to us. Regardless of the crisis or circumstances, God's reasons are beyond our comprehension. It only took me a few short lessons to not ask God such questions anymore. Instead, I accepted that I have no control over my life and trust whatever happens, He will work it out for my good. This perception not only helps keep me one hundred yards from a straight jacket, it provides peace knowing that God is in control and all things are in His hands.

God has provided peace for thousands of years and leads us back to a man in the book of Judges by the name of Gideon. Not only was his clan the weakest of all the clans, he was also the runt of the litter. During his lifetime, the Israelites were hiding under rocks and in caves because of the oppression of the Midianites. Can you imagine feeling two inches tall, hiding in dark caves, always looking over your shoulder, and wondering if you're going to live the rest of the day? Gideon was one such character. He was hiding out in a winepress to thresh wheat when an angel of the Lord appeared to him. God decided to build trust in this little man. The message to Gideon was something totally out of character and unexpected. (Review Judges 6 to read the story.) God was calling him to lead his nation out of the mess they were in. Still unsure of this heavenly stranger, Gideon wanted to be sure of his credentials and asked the angel to perform a miracle. When the meat and bread were consumed by a heavenly fire, Gideon was terrified, until the angel of the Lord stated, "Peace! Do not be afraid. You are not going to die" (Judges 6:23). After this supernatural encounter, Gideon built an altar to the Lord and called it "The Lord is Peace."

My crisis may be little compared to Gideon's, but God did not even hesitate to wrap me in a blanket of tranquility and calm during my moment of need. Terrified or not, He is at the ready to stand with you. Crisis or stress He wants to share peace with you. Teething baby or angry tween, God is at the ready to cover your life in His hands of peace.

More often than not when I am anxious, upset, or just plain irritated I have to remind myself to ask God for peace that transcends all understanding. Let your mind dwell on God. Read His Word and hide His words in your heart. Recall them when you are ready to pull your hair out. Remember them when life brings you to your knees (it's a good position to receive the fullest from God anyway). Recite them when your child is working on your last nerve. More often than not, God will center your emotions and perception on His love for you and the worries you have will fade into the calm that is rising up in you.

After I let go and surrendered my baby boy to God, things took a turn for the better. Four months later at Elijah's checkup, he was a whopping twenty-six pounds. He had rolls on top of rolls. His weight gain made his doctor regret her words and she was awed when the x-rays came back normal. The heart murmur was gone. It was like God was showing off His awesome powers. He had control over Elijah's life. All I needed to do was let go and trust in God. Mama's milk and prayers were the things he needed to thrive.

Mama's Time-Out

What is the first thing you do when life sweeps you off your feet? Do you call a friend or talk to your husband? If so, it's time to revise your crisis strategies. Today take the time to pick out a few favorite verses that calm your heart and memorize them. Next teach them to your little ones. Recite your verses for them daily so that they too learn to turn to God.

Today's Love Note

*Do not be anxious about anything,
but in every situation, by prayer and petition,
with thanksgiving, present your requests to God.
And the peace of God, which transcends all understanding,
will guard your hearts and your minds in Christ Jesus.*

Philippians 4:6-7

I Call Him By Name

Yahweh Shalom, Your name means more than peace. It means dwelling within me and restoring me to wholeness. It means life is in Your capable hands. As I come before you today, I ask that I am touched by Your presence of peace. With the situation I am facing, I ask to be able to see Your hand in it. I want Your presence to calm my heart. I pray that Your love blankets me and casts out all worries and fears. Thank You for Your Word and the lessons of peace that dwell within these pages. In Your name Yahweh Shalom, I pray. Amen.

Be Still

Be still? Fat chance; I'm hardly ever still, although there have been many days while being in the trenches of motherhood that I wished I could have waved the white flag and surrendered to being still. Have I mentioned that my younger two children are independent, emotional, and strong willed? The only chance I get to be still is when they are sleeping; even then I'm trying to catch my breath. Only this morning while still in bed, I could hear screams of injustice penetrate my dream-clouded wonderland. Apparently, Tori took Elijah's toy skateboard, she not only took it, and she also clobbered him with a large truck while running off with her loot. This type of thing happens every five minutes, *all day long.* It seems that Tori's sole purpose in life besides looking cute with her strawberry blond, blue-eyed features is to also make her brother miserable . . . every second of the day.

As chaotic and irritating as my children can be, there is a peace and calm that floods my heart and home. Back to the B.C. (Before Christ) days, I was paranoid, nervous, stressed out, fidgety and needed at least seven different medications to keep me feeling and acting sane. Even though I only had one child, life itself seemed to toss me about in a sea of frenzy.

Nothing calmed my mind and there was a constant storm brewing within in my soul. I danced on the edge of eternity, sensing life wasn't supposed to be lived like this. Of course it didn't help that I was seeing a counselor three times a week to revisit childhood issues and other traumas. The storm I was in came with plenty of labels. Bi-polar Disorder, Manic Depression, Post Traumatic Stress Disorder, and Borderline Personality Disorder (this one has become a favorite because as mothers we all become borderline due to lack of sleep and monstrous two year olds), hence the need for the medication. I needed medication to keep my moods level, then I needed another pill to keep my focus, another for paranoia, another for anxiety and still another to fall asleep.

After I gave my life to Christ, I was invited to a Bible study with Angela Loven (a.k.a spiritual sister and B.F.F). For all purposes of her name, she embodied the love of Christ for His people. Our relationship involved several fights which included messages left on our answering machines. Our husbands reluctantly became involved, relaying what the other said.

"Heather, Angela called," Chris would say with a deep sigh. "She wants to know if you're still mad at her?"

"I'm not mad, I'm ticked!" I'd reply. "Call her back and tell her to give me some breathing room!" I'd yell from the bedroom.

Chris would then call and tell Lance (Angela's husband) what my answer was; in turn, he would tell Angela. Through the test of time, she has managed to demonstrate true friendship and what it looks like to truly walk with Christ. Each time I entered her home, I craved the peace and calmness that I could see radiating from her.

So what does a baby Christian do when she is in need of a lifestyle makeover? She becomes an imitator of those walking in faith. Sure, there was a peace that flooded into my heart that night I said yes to Jesus, but I still needed more. I began imitating what I saw my best friend doing. So I began reading the Bible every day, praying, and begging God to mold me into what He wanted me to be. I cried out to have the life He intended for me (some days I wonder about this decision, mainly, when I'm elbow deep in poop or when I think my eardrums busted from all the screaming). I watched how Angela treated her husband, took notes of her mother skills, and how she interacted with those around her.

True peace was found when I completely surrendered all control of my life to Christ. Keep in mind that surrendering isn't a one-time thing. It's something that I must do daily; otherwise my control-freak nature tends to take over. When I began to surrender my all, I could truly taste and sense Yahweh Shalom. Shalom is a Hebrew word that refers to the absence of conflict or an inner state of calm. It means wholeness, safety, completeness, wellness, soundness and complete satisfaction. It comes from living in harmony with God. Living in harmony in God requires that we surrender all. We yield our thoughts, actions, dreams, and children to the care and control of God. This is a tall order; it's crucial in our walk with God and to have some sort of sanity while raising kids.

Gideon referred to God as the *Lord is Peace,* by building a stone monument, this title has become one of the most well-known characteristics about Christ and one of the most favorites. Peace reigns upon the hearts of those who love Christ, and I believe it's more visible in women. As mothers, we are acquainted with peace intimately as it is a part of our design. Not that I'm criticizing our manly counterparts, or saying that we were made to be barefoot, pregnant, and in the kitchen; we were created with a different intuition.

The peace of God radiates from every single Christian no matter the circumstances. Regardless of the chaos which is a constant undercurrent in your home (and for every other mother in this nation with preschoolers), or some other life circumstance that has hit you below the belt, there is peace. Peace soothes and calms our minds. It acts as a balm to soothe our frustrated hearts. It grants serenity to a fragile, sleep-deprived mind. It invades life traumas quietly but the effects are transforming.

Your present situation may be that you are searching for peace. Maybe you've learned you have breast cancer, your husband lost his job, or your child is failing all his/her classes. It could be the economy knocking on your door, threatening your mortgage payments. Or it could simply be your family doesn't yet know our God. Sit down and talk to God. It doesn't have to be fancy, just modest. Ask God for a hedge of protection around your home and ask for peace to flood the space. Pray and surrender it all. Grant Him control and thank Him for loving you. Pray as anxiety threatens the barricades of your mind. Teach the prayer to your children and sing it through your day. Dear mama, before you know it, God's gift of peace will flood your heart and your mind. Your worries and prayers will be present on His altar as Jesus advocates for you. So take a break, take a little rest, maybe take a bubble bath and talk to God. (The bath may require duck taping your children's rears to the couch and ear plugs for your own ears.)

Mama's Time-Out

- What areas of your life do you sense need a makeover? Is it your faith in God, trust in others, or maybe you have some labels you'd like to get rid of?

- Evaluate what those things are and then take them to God. Share this with your husband or close friend and begin taking the steps to find peace within. Blessings to you on this journey!

Today's Love Note

*For this is what the L*ORD *says: "I will extend peace to her like a river, and the wealth of nations like a flooding stream; you will nurse and be carried on her arm and dandled on her knees."*

Isaiah 66:12

I Call Him By Name

As a woman and a mom it is so hard to be still. Yahweh Shalom, I ask for calm to flood my heart and my home. I pray that Your name and Your peace cast out all anxious thoughts and all busyness that take me away from Your presence. You know my heart and my thoughts. You know my worries, insecurities, and the activity level of my home. Bring peace to my life. Let it blanket this home, and my heart. Amen.

YAHWEH NISSI

The Lord Is My Banner

Exodus 17:8-16; Song of Songs 2:4; Isaiah 49:22-25

*Start children off on the way they should go,
and even when they are old they will not turn from it.*

Proverbs 22:6

Raising Up Soldiers

There is a war brewing in America. The battle lines are being drawn and it's starting in our schools. The primary targets are the minds of our children. We can no longer freely say, *"One nation under God."* Children are discouraged from praying during lunch. Symbols of their faith are considered contraband because they may be offensive to others. Laws are being passed saying that the public schools are to teach our children that they should accept and tolerate homosexual relationships. Books are available in their libraries that teach God as some magic being like Santa Claus.

There are many aspects and battlefronts to this war but the primary war is between Christianity and secular humanism. Secular humanism is a religion and philosophy of life which views man as the supreme being of the world. God and all the supernatural "stuff" is mere fluff. It sees moral values as relative and varying from person to person. These morals are personable until the individual decides to change them, so long as it doesn't hurt anybody else. We live in a day and age where double standards are acceptable and Christianity is considered intolerant.

For several weeks my husband and I went back and forth over pulling our oldest daughter out of public school and putting her into a private Christian school. We were alarmed what she was being taught to tolerate in school and concerned with legislative standards passing as law in California.

Our decision became clear after a bullying incident on the last day of school. Because my neighbor and I carpooled, Chy often came home with the Machard boys. While Chy and Justin were waiting for Pauline, this group of kids teased them about being more than friends. The teasing went from words to physical altercations of being pinched. Chy came home with bruises on her ears. Cheyenne has such a tender heart, besides not understanding social cues through her Asperger's. We felt she needed a place to blossom without the fear of getting teased. With this incident, we felt private education was the best place for our little girl.

Some parents would view our decision as sheltering our child; still other parents feel children need to be in the public setting to shine their light for Christ. We agree with both perspectives, but we felt God was calling Chy to be placed in a private Christian school, not only for her education and self-esteem but to give her a stronger foundation in the Bible. Our faith is strong, but we are still new in Christ, and sometimes we are barely a step ahead of her! Most of the time we are learning right alongside of her. Her new school does just that. It sparks conversations and leads us to debate with our Bibles in hand. As she encounters Christ's Word, it is building up her faith and reinforcing her armor she puts on daily as she walks out the door. It has raised the standard in our home, and that standard is to live for Christ.

In the Bible the word "standard" was translated in many texts to mean banner. A banner is just that, a standard. In ancient days, banners were carved on wood and metals to represent a clan or nations ideals. This banner or flag could be seen from a distance and was often a rallying point for troops just before battle. It was raised high during critical times in the battle to boost the soldiers' morale, to help them find their strength and remind them what they were fighting for.

My dear little mama, it's all coming down to the final wire, the final battle. In these last days, you and I both need to decide how we are going to raise our children. If I'm not mistaken, you love Christ and the choice is clear. It's time to raise our banners high so others can see that we serve Christ. We serve a God who does not tolerate double standards and will not make light of how society has discredited Him and His kingdom.

It may seem like we are losing this battle, but don't forget what Yahweh Nissi means. Yahweh Nissi means "The Lord is My Banner." Read Exodus 17 when Moses raised his staff as a banner that God was with Israelites in the midst of battle. It was their first battle after being freed from Egypt. His brother and sister helped keep the staff in the air after Moses' arms grew heavy.

After their enemies were defeated, Moses built an altar and called God *our banner*. When you pray and call on Yahweh Nissi, you are calling on a God who is powerful enough to overcome any foe, and that includes the enemy who disguises himself as secular humanism.

The battlefield may at times look bleak; keep in mind Yahweh Nissi is shining His light over our children. Start teaching your children how to put on their armor and pray for their safety each day before they go off to play or head off to school. Finally, let your banner be raised high so it can be seen from a distance as an encouragement to those who are fighting in this battle with us.

Mama's Time-Out

Put on the armor of God (Ephesians 6:10-17)

Yahweh Nissi, thank You for today and I ask that You watch over my family as we go about our day. Help me to put on my armor so that I am protected and can stand up in the battle. First, I pray that You help me protect my mind with the helmet of salvation. Help me to make right decisions. Next, I pray that You protect my heart with the breastplate of righteousness. I ask forgiveness for my sins that I may be found pardoned in Your eyes. Help me to obey Your voice and Your Word. Next, I pray for help to remember that You are truth as I put on the belt of truth. It will help remind me of all that I know about You. Also, I pray that as I put on my sandals of peace that You'll guide my feet on the path they should go. Help me to carry my shield of faith as it will help protect me from doubt and keep the enemy away. And last, I pray You help me carry the sword of the Spirit which is Your Word. Use it to guide my way today and every day. In Jesus' name, amen.

Today's Love Note

"See I will beckon to the Gentiles,
I will lift up my banner to the peoples;
they will bring your son in their arms
and carry your daughters on their shoulders....
Then you will know that I am the LORD;
those who hope in me will not be disappointed."
Can plunder be taken from warriors,
or captives rescued from the fierce?
But this is what the LORD says:

> "Yes, captives will be taken from warriors,
> And plunder retrieved from the fierce,
> I will contend with those who contend with you,
> and your children I will save."
>
> Isaiah 49:22-25

I Call Him By Name

Yahweh Nissi, prepare my heart and the hearts of my children for what is to come. I call on Your mighty name to shield my children when they are in school. I pray that Your banner waves fiercely over them, and that no foe will want to contend with You or Your children. In Your Son's precious name. Amen.

Where I Belong

Here in Nebraska nearly every banner waving during the football season is red. The townspeople are a sea of red, black, and white shirts with the Cornhusker logo. And the connection of supporting the Cornhuskers unites punk college kids and grandpas alike. It's obvious the Cornhuskers are everybody's banner of choice. If you don't root for the Huskers, expect to have your house toilet-papered and decorated with the colors of the big red phenomenon. Even children are dressed in Husker jerseys or red and white pleated cheerleader outfits. (These are staple items at our local Walmart.)

 I haven't gotten used to the whole Husker-love thing (I own nothing Husker), mainly because I was never a big fan of sports and never really felt a sense of belonging for as long as I can remember. Since childhood, I have been an outcast. For various reasons during those early years, I was set afloat in the sea of life, but merely drifting. In school it was hard to identify with any clique because I wasn't pretty enough, rebellious, athletic, or smart enough. I spent my life drifting from one crowd to the next trying to fit in. When we moved from the fast-paced city of Tucson, Arizona, to small-town Newcastle, Wyoming, I felt like a goose in a henhouse of chickens. My disdain of dirt, smelly animals, and being anti-rodeo didn't help my predicament. Rodeos and branding cows weren't my forte at all! (The climate change was shocking enough, not to mention a new way of life: Redneckville. Can you blame a snotty city girl for that kind of thinking? Now I miss Newcastle.) Even in the throes of motherhood, I still had a hard time identifying with anyone. Granted I was seventeen when I first became a mother.

It wasn't until I came to know Christ in my early twenties that I found my place in this world. Being adopted into Christ's family gave me everything I was searching for. It provided ownership, love, friendship common ground, purpose, and values. It defined what Christ created me and called me to be. All of it was united under the banner of hope. As Bible-thumperish (yes, it's a word) as it sounds, Christ unites us all under the banner of hope. It's a banner that penetrates the loneliest of souls and adopts us into a family far greater than we can imagine.

You may be like me and spent years trying to fit in, or you may have a child who is struggling to find herself in school. It's agonizing watching your child try and fail in all those areas that you may have excelled at. Or maybe you can identify feeling the way your child does. My daughter Cheyenne spent the first few years of her life looking for a banner other crowds carried that she could perceive as her own.

She is compassionate, loving, silly, and very tall. She has curly blond locks and glasses that cover her big hazel-brown eyes. She likes to play games but not sports. She loves to play with friends, but only as long as she gets to create or imagine some new magical world. She is a walking encyclopedia of animal and science facts but struggles to maintain good grades because of her learning disability. Yet, in her new school setting, she fits in because she is a part of God's family. The funny thing about God is He likes, maybe even favors, variety. Is there any other Cheyenne in this world? No. Is there any other you in this world? Again the answer is no. Look at the stars. Each is different; each shines its own dazzling light as God calls it into existence. Each snowflake or grain of sand is different; millions are created, yet no two are alike. Our world looks for comparisons, trying to make everyone and everything fit in a standard or category. Like these grains of sand and stars, it was time to find a place for Cheyenne to shine for God.

Once we plucked her from public school and placed her in private school, it allowed her to bloom into what God intended her to be. She found friends who love her for who she is. She now has a best friend that finishes her sentences and speaks for her, and they are united under the banner of Christ! Cheyenne had prayed for years to find a good and faithful friend, and God totally went beyond her expectations!

Scripture tell us over and over that those who hope in God will not be disappointed. As a mom you may be struggling with finding yourself and where you fit in. Believe it or not, I am accepted by friends at my church and other groups even though I'm feisty, loud-mouthed, and have tattoos. They all are aware of my background and still love me for me. They enjoy walking beside me along the journey Christ has for me.

If you are still struggling with these concepts, remember there is a banner uniting you in God's family. The common ground is your children, your love for Christ, and how God made you for a purpose. I encourage you to find a group to belong to. You'll be able to bloom under the banner of Christ. You don't have to be a Husker fan to find a few good friends. Check out what your church offers or ask a few friends!

Mama's Time-Out

- What causes you to be wary of forming friendships?

- Do you identify with Christ's banner?

- If you are looking for a group, MOPS International (Mothers of Preschoolers) is one I highly recommend. Go to www.mops.org to find a local group in your area.

- Another group is Hearts at Home. www.hearts-at-home.org

- If prayer is your kind of thing, then check out www.momsintouch.org

- Other ideas to help you identify with Christ are checking out what your church offers in terms of groups and Bible studies. Join a young moms group!

Today's Love Note

In that day the Root of Jesse will stand as a banner for the peoples;
the nations will rally to him, and his resting place will be glorious.
In that day the Lord will reach out his hand a second time to reclaim the surviving
remnant of his people from Assyria, from Lower Egypt,
from Upper Egypt, from Cush, from Elam, from Babylonia,
from Hamath and from the islands of the Mediterranean.
He will raise a banner for the nations and gather the exiles of Israel;
he will assemble the scattered people of Judah
from the four quarters of the earth.

Isaiah 11:10-12

I Call Him By Name

Yahweh Nissi, my heart is lonely and unsure of where it belongs. Show me and remind me that I belong to You. Raise up Your banner of love over me. I pray my heart finds its home in You. I know You understand the depths of my heart as I come before Your throne. Amen.

ISH

Husband

Hosea 2:16; Isaiah 54:5-8; 62:4-5

*Even the sparrow has found a home, and
the swallow a nest for herself, where she may have her young—
a place near your altar, Lord Almighty, my King and my God.*

Psalm 84:3

All the Single Ladies

"I just don't think I can do this anymore," Tiffany sobbed on my front porch. "I mean look at me. I'm almost twenty-six years old and I'm back home living with my parents because I failed to make a life for us in Oklahoma."

Without saying a word I just hugged her. Tiffany had been struggling with feelings of guilt and failure after moving back to Kearney because she was unable to find a good job to support her four-year-old daughter and herself. Normally Tiffany and I don't hug; usually we rub each other the wrong way. But for lack of better words, we make each other stronger. I point out her flaws while she points out mine. When we haven't felt the need to kill each other and are able to dine out for sushi, the perspective the other offers gives us grace and room for growth. She reminds me each morning as she drops off her daughter before rushing off to work to be thankful for my husband and the fact that I get to be a stay-at-home mom. Each day I remind her that though the road she is traveling is tough, God is with her.

Tiffany is a single mom who has the world on her shoulders. She has an education, but she struggles to make ends meet and dreams of being a stay-at-home mom for her daughter. Instead, she works as a para-professional at the local high school. This wasn't supposed to be the plan. She honestly thought her boyfriend would come through on all he promised. Instead, he left her by the wayside, leaving Tiffany to clean up the mess and attempt to explain to her ever inquisitive daughter why she doesn't have a daddy. Like most single moms,

Tiffany is praying for a husband who will be more than she ever dreamed of. This man will not only have to meet Tiffany's desires but Keely's as well. While researching data for this chapter, I asked her what the toughest part about navigating parental territory solo was.

"I don't think it is the day-to-day life, like everyone assumes. If that was the hardest, it would be unmanageable and impossible. Single moms are strong and fierce. If they are not, they don't stay single but end up in bad relationship after bad relationship (usually). Sometimes it is really hard, especially when comparing myself with friends. Especially when they think they understand because they never possibly could. They might understand financially or emotionally or physically or spiritually but never all of it at the same time. These aspects compound into something that you can't appreciate unless you have been there. That makes single motherhood a very lonely place sometimes."

Sadly enough, there are more single moms out there then one might imagine. It used to be a rare thing until the last two decades. It's unmistakably becoming common. According to the U. S. Census Bureau, there are about 13.7 million single parents in the United States today and they are responsible for raising 21.8 million children. Of these numbers, 84 percent are moms. That means about one in four children are being raised in a single-parent home. Mamas who are single not only raise their children, they work forty-plus hours per week, make sure the house duties are kept, cook 100 percent of the meals, help with homework, and ensure all needs are met for their children (Jennifer Wolf. *Single Parent Statistics*. About.com).

Whether you're single by choice or by a series of unintentional events, the results are the same. You've been given the greatest gift in the world. You've been given the chance to comprehend in some small way how God feels about us as His children. You get to experience the joy when a milestone is reached and the grief of wrong choices made by your child. Yet at the same time, single moms feel judged, misunderstood, and are just plain tired! Single mamas have the entire world resting on their shoulders. This burden of responsibility should have been divided and resting on two sets of shoulders. Their common companion is worry. The restless nights include thoughts of how to show their child that he or she is loved, cared for, wanted. The other ever constant thought that consumes their thought life is the concern of how their child will turn out compared to children from two-parent homes. Here is a post from Cassidy, a high school classmate and friend, as she worries about her son:

> The biggest challenges to single parenting are money and time.

I have to work full time and cannot pick my son up at school, so I only see him in the evenings and every other weekend when he has visits with his paternal family. My fears about raising a good Christian son are that life outside in the secular world does not accept being a good person a lot of times. You have to lie, cheat, etc. I want him to have the love of Christ in his heart and know that love when he interacts with others. My fear is that he will and can walk away from his faith because of the challenges we have faced. I do not want him to blame God for the struggles, which I know all kids do at times, but fear he will not understand that God never promised that bad things would not happen, but he would walk with us when they did.

My dear little single mama, God wants just as much goodness and abundance in your life as He does for married mamas. You are still raising His children. When you came into a relationship with Christ, He vowed to be yours forever and ever. Not sure what I'm talking about? He is your Ish. Ish is the Hebrew word for husband. It is the perfect reflection of His love for His people and commitment to them. He is the perfect husband. He is loving and true. He is your protector, provider, and companion during those long lonely nights. God makes this passion and love for us more apparent when He reveals Jesus as the bridegroom in the New Testament. His Son was given for the love of His church.

God was first introduced as Ish in the Bible in the book of Hosea. In this book, God tells Hosea to find and marry a prostitute. (Not my idea of marriage... but then I tend to be the jealous type.) Hosea obeys and marries a prostitute who leaves him time and again for her other lovers and lust for material things. Hosea's life becomes a living representation of God's love for His people. His people wonder away from Him and commit adulterous acts by worshipping other idols and allowing the sinful nature of their desires pervert the covenant between themselves and God. Instead of throwing us out on our backsides for cheating on Him, God portrays His love through us as Hosea did for his wife. He went after Gomer time and again and even "wooed" her back into the relationship. This metaphor shows that God is forgiving and loving. He provides all our needs. He is our protector even when we walk away.

Little mama, don't let the enemy get to your heart. He is filling you with lies and guilt about the situation you are in. Whether you are a single mom by divorce, widowhood, or other choices, it does not matter. God loves you so deeply and intimately, He wants to be known as Ish to you. He wants you to know this, you have a partner in life and in parenting. His name is Christ. While you may become weary over this huge responsibility, you are never alone. He is there. He wants you to succeed and your children to flourish. He is there to support and guide you every step of the way.

Mama's Time-Out

As a single mom, it's especially important to know the promises God has given you in His Word. Here are a few I've listed that you can jot down and remember what He wants for you as your Ish.

- "Ask and it will be given to you; seek and you will find; knock and the door will be opened to you. For everyone who asks receives; the one who seeks finds; and to the one who knocks, the door will be opened" (Matthew 7:7-8).

- "I can do all this through him who gives me strength" (Philippians 4:13).

- "Whoever fears the LORD has a secure fortress, and for their children it will be a refuge" (Proverbs 14:26).

- "Keep his decrees and commands, which I am giving you today, so that it may go well with you and your children after you and that you may live long in the land the LORD your God gives you for all time" (Deuteronomy 4:40).

Today's Love Note

"In that day," declares the LORD, "you will call me 'my husband';
you will no longer call me 'my master.'...
I will betroth you to me forever;
I will betroth you in righteousness and justice, in love and compassion.
I will betroth you in faithfulness,
and you will acknowledge the LORD."

Hosea 2:16, 19-20

I Call Him By Name

To know that You want to be my husband is indescribable. It floods my heart with uncontainable joy. The knowledge Your Word has spoken to my spirit is too much for me to take in. I pray that You will draw me in deeper to You. To know that You want to pursue a relationship with me floods my heart with joy. Help me to remember to cling to this promise when times are tough. Help me to remember Your Word when my children are asking about their daddy. Give me the strength to parent the children You've given me to the best of my ability. Take my heart, for it is Yours so that I can freely call You Ish. In Your Son's name. Amen.

The Seven-Year Itch
(Four Years Later)

Overnight I became a single mom. My husband's career had become more demanding as he traveled all over the world to conquer grain bin issues. He's even been all the way to Russia, just to ensure 30 million dollars worth of grain bins were built correctly. Plus traveling to Kentucky just to take a picture of a blown-over grain bin to officially say, "Yep, it's busted."

Not only has his career become more demanding, he made the decision to go back to school to pursue a degree in business. While my dear husband decided to go back to school to provide a better life for us, he also did it so he doesn't have to deal with angry rednecks and Canadians on a daily basis (which also meant I got to repeat college by doing some of his homework and essays; I currently have a B average).

This left me with all the responsibilities of running our home and parenting our children. (Have I mentioned how crazy my children are?) While it may not seem like a big deal, Chris's absence seemed to drive me over the edge as I experienced a whole new definition of lonely. Then, as if the enemy enjoyed playing devil's advocate with me, an old friend from the B.C. days resurfaced. (Many of us have these skeletons in our closet; they however don't feel the need to make an example of themselves like mine unfortunately do.) This friend whom we will call John Doe was engaged to be married and had just gotten back from serving over in Afghanistan. (We lost touch after I gave my life to Christ.) The conversations started out innocently enough from catching up to reminiscing about the old days.

Soon I was talking to him more than my husband. Text messages, phone calls, and emails, until one day he wanted more than I ever expected him to ask of me. He wanted more than what I could give, and it was time to tell my husband. Though I didn't physically cheat, the fact that I had a past connection with a non-Christian man was more than my husband could bear. I had clearly made the right choice to cut off all contact with John; however, I still reaped the consequences of my actions and it left a void in my heart that was relentless. I was more isolated, shamed, and lonelier than ever. It wasn't until I heard God's voice at a women's retreat that I understood why that void was there (and why Satan was able to play me like a fiddle).

It was this particular moment as I was sitting alone in my seat at the women's retreat that I knew God was ready to scoop me back up into His arms. My heart had been aching for so long from loneliness and insecurity that I stopped hearing His voice. Unknowingly, I had begun to look for something more tangible to fill it.

"I'll take these chains, this bondage, and ransom you. Abandon your heart, your desires, and let Me come to you. I am moving. You may not see Me, but I am conquering in the spirit. I'm still right here where I always was. You, Heather, must return to Me for Me to heal you. My heart is breaking for you as you go through this, but there is so much glory, honor, and victory once you arrive on the other side."

I was in complete awe of how His words were romancing my heart. That void in my heart was gone; it was full of Him. I continued to sit, humbled by His presence and His words to me.

"I will be your Ish. I will give you the intimacy you crave, the romance you long for. For I created you, and only the Master can make you complete. I gave you the longing for attention because I want to fill it. I want to love you more than any man can here on this earth. I know the depths of your heart, the longing in your soul, and the need to be completely loved. Only I can love and cherish you in a way that is inexhaustible. I want to pursue your heart, to prize it above all others. All others will forsake you, yes, even the man that I placed by your side will not love you as much as I. Just remember that I created you. I, alone, am completely captivated by the depth of your beauty, every heartbeat, every thought, and every breath you take. Even the scars you bear. I love you so deeply and know you so

intimately that there is no end of Me and no beginning of you. Even when you wander, I will be here waiting, ready to embrace you."

Imagine, the God of the universe telling you that He loves you and is *captivated* by you. I decided to share this very personal experience and intimate moments with you, little mama, because I know what it's like to be married and still feel alone. I know the constant gnawing on your heart, but so does God. He created us to be relational creatures, so jabbering with a two year old and a four year old doesn't exactly fill the need we have. One of the most fascinating word images of God is as a husband. God wants us to look to Him first and fill our needs with His time and His Word and then look to our husbands to fill the rest. Though, in our eyes, a marriage is considered as a promise of vows by two people, it takes three to make it work. The third person is God.

Marriage is found in almost all cultures and its institution is described throughout the Bible in several ways. Ideas from how a man should care for his wife, to how a wife should submit to her husband, to Jesus described as a bridegroom and the church as His bride. Marriage was not only a way to populate the earth but was designed by God to meet the need we have for sharing our lives together. Through our marriages, we learn what it truly means to love, cherish, forgive, and sacrifice for our spouse and through our children that come from our marriage. Going back to Hosea, we see how God loves faithless Israel and draws her back time and again through the marriage of Hosea and Gomer. Where Hosea fails, God steps in. When Gomer runs after her lovers, God again steps in, with these words, *"Therefore I am now going to allure her; I will lead her into the wilderness and speak tenderly to her"* (Hosea 2:14).

Instead of being jealous and angry with Gomer and Israel, God instead whispers kind words and reveals the depth of His forgiveness and love. He also showed me this at the retreat. Though I made some pretty big mistakes, He knows how lonely parenting can be. Not just for me but for every woman. God wants to make it perfectly clear to us that we are *never* alone. His presence is ever with us, His words ever ready to speak to our hearts.

Mama's Time Out

- Marriage is becoming a past tradition in today's culture. It's not respected like it once was. Examine your marriage and begin protecting it in ways that apply for you and your husband. Because I want to protect my relationship, I safeguard it. I will not talk to another man for more than five minutes alone, even if I'm at Walmart.

- Attend a Weekend To Remember Marriage Retreat. They are sponsored by Family Life. Visit Familylife.com
- Safeguard and strengthen your marriage by communicating with your husband. Tell him your thoughts, needs, and fears. Demonstrate what a healthy marriage looks like in front of your children.
- Pick up the book, *Love and Respect* by Dr. Emerson Eggerichs or *The Love Dare* by Stephen Kendrick and Alex Kendrick.

Today's Love Note

For your Maker is your husband—the LORD Almighty is his name—the Holy One of Israel is your Redeemer; he is called the God of all the earth. The LORD will call you back as if you were a wife deserted and distressed in spirit— a wife who married young, only to be rejected," says your God. "For a brief moment I abandoned you, but with deep compassion I will bring you back. In a surge of anger I hid my face from you for a moment, but with everlasting kindness I will have compassion on you," says the LORD your Redeemer.

Isaiah 54:5-8

I Call Him By Name

Ish, You know how busy our lives have become. You know the sacrifice it takes in these times for our husbands to provide. You also know the toll an absent husband can take on a wife. God, I come before You and ask for blessings of Your presence with me as I read Your Word. I pray You alone will fill the gap that my husband cannot. I call on Your name as Ish to be my husband. Help me to look to You and fill my cup with Your presence and Your Word so that loneliness is not a battle for me, but a victory in Your presence. Amen.

SHOPPET

The Lord Is My Judge

Psalm 94:2-15; Matthew 7:1-6; Romans 2:1-4

*"Do not judge, or you too will be judged.
For in the same way you judge others, you will be judged,
and with the measure you use, it will be measured to you."*

MATTHEW 7:1-2

The Ultimate Judge

Most days in my home, I have not one judge but three. Tori (my little spitfire has a short fuse and big temper—she resembles a firecracker or dynamite) is usually the one who imparts judgment on her brother or daycare kids if they do something that offends her, which is often. Oh so often, maybe thirty times a day. Have you been there? I'll pray for you! For example, Cole decided not to include Tori in the game he was playing with his Batman and cars. Against better judgment, he grabbed all the toys and turned his back on her. Tori stood there for a moment, as if deciding what doom she would bestow on the poor boy, and then she let him have it. Before Cole could blink, she throttled him with her little hands and bit his back before walking away. Cole was a mess of tears and traumatized that a little girl, half his size and age, had beat him up.

Finally the real judge had to step in, no not Tori—me! After explaining to Cole that he needed to include Tori and all their friends in playing together, I then bestowed my judgment on Tori for clobbering and biting Cole.

As moms we are constantly judging actions, words, work, play, and even thoughts (I can see what my children are thinking; this is just another mommy skill I've honed to my advantage). Most days it gets on my nerves when I have to deal with the same offense fifty times over (welcome to the terrible twos . . . and threes . . . and yes . . . the fours). While it would just be easier to tell them to knock it off and discipline them, instead I take the time to remind them that Jesus is watching. Again I repeat the golden rule of kindness. I care about what my children do now because it's in these first few years they are moldable and malleable. Their minds and character are in my hands.

It's my job to ignore the minor details of chores and focus on building morals and godly character. Trust me—the laundry will always be there, my kids won't be, especially in this impressionable state. Picking my battles isn't easy; there have been a few that have left me defeated. But I stand firm in discipline in terms of character building, morals, and values. I'm also the type of parent who has wild daydreams over the smallest of offenses that balloon into major offenses when my child becomes an adult. I've seen my son in jail clothes over sneaking a piece of candy; it's not pretty.

I'm afraid if I give in just a little or let something go now, the long run may prove my lack of parental skills and will cause the law to impart judgment on my children's character. Not sure what I'm talking about? Case in point: Review Eli and his two wayward sons that God killed for their less-than-stellar actions. "And the LORD said to Samuel: 'See, I am about to do something in Israel that will make the ears of everyone who hears of it tingle. At that time I will carry out against Eli everything I spoke against his family—from beginning to end. For I told him that I would judge his family forever because of the sin he knew about; his sons made themselves contemptible, and he failed to restrain them. Therefore, I swore to the house of Eli, "The guilt of Eli's house will never be atoned for by sacrifice or offering"'" (1 Samuel 3:11-14).

Eli's sons were priests and treated sacrifices with disrespect not to mention they slept with the women who took care of the Tent Gates. Eli knew about their actions and chose not to rebuke or pull them from their positions in the temple. Because he chose not to carry out judgment (via discipline) against his children, God did it for him in the worst way. They all lost their lives, including Eli. Eli must have thought he was showing them mercy. Maybe he was thinking his boys were good boys, but they were just making poor choices or maybe it was just a phase and they would snap out of it. Because Eli ignored his responsibility of correcting his children, they all paid the ultimate price; they lost their lives.

Thankfully you and I are not like Eli. If you are reading this book, it's because you need some quiet time and a few good laughs over my parenting debacles; but, mainly you're reading this because you want to know *who* God really is. You want to embrace all aspects of His character and reveal Him to your children. The world has pushed God into the background, and no longer is everything in varying shades of grey. And while we continue on in this fashion, God is still waiting to impart judgment on every soul on this earth. Shoppet is a Hebrew verb that is translated in various synonyms throughout the Good Book including, judge, govern, defend, deliver, decide, and vindicate (Larry Richards, *Encyclopedia of Bible Words*).

We hold God in awesome reverence to think of Him as not only our Defender, Refuge, or Father, but the idea of revering Him as Judge causes me to shudder. Imagine for a moment that He is standing in the room with you. This reminds us that though God may not be standing here physically right now, we will be standing before Him one day having to answer for our actions. It reminds us that His righteousness demands justice, and not just any justice, but the perfect ultimate justice. Though these thoughts may scare you, remember He's provided a way out of our imperfections and sin through His Son. Need another reminder that He is full of love as well as justice? Isaiah 30:18 says, "Yes the LORD longs to be gracious to you; he rises to show you compassion. For the LORD is a God of justice. Blessed are those who wait for him!" Now this doesn't mean you need to beat your child into submission; nor does it mean we are to ridicule or treat our children harshly either. That type of parenting means you need to get help.

A parent who disciplines as a way to get back at her child is a parent who needs some professional help. It may sound as if I'm mocking you, but I'm not. I've seen too many children cringe from their parents in the supermarket and many more whose hearts have no hope left. The early years are when our children are most impressionable. The last thing your child needs to be filled with is shame and fear of his mom or dad. Instead, treat your child with compassion as Christ treats you even now. Granted it may take giving yourself a time out before you deal with your child, so do so!

More times than I can count, I've placed Elijah (my impulsive boy, full of spunk) in his room while I went to my room to calm down. I would root out the issue of why I was so angry, pray God to help me deal with it, then go back and deal with my child with proper judgment by looking through Christ's eyes at my son. It's through our hands, actions, and hearts that our children will gain a sense of who God is. Not only are we to teach them He is full of love, that He is sovereign, but that He is also the ultimate Judge. By your hands and His grace we can lead them to love Him as our Judge, the One who will justify us in our time of need as well.

Mama's Time-Out

- Pretend for a day that Jesus is standing next you, and He is recording everything you say, do or think. At the end of the day, review how your behavior changed (or didn't). Are you thankful that God has pardoned you already?

- Here are a few Scriptures to review the next time you care tempted to be the judge: James 4:12; John 8:15-16; 12:47-49; 1 Peter 4:5; 2 Timothy 4:1, 8.

Today's Love Note

For God did not send his Son into the world to condemn the world, but to save the world through him. Whoever believes in him is not condemned, but whoever does not believe stands condemned already because they have not believed in the name of God's one and only Son. This is the verdict: Light has come into the world, but people loved darkness instead of light because their deeds were evil. Everyone who does evil hates the light, and will not come into the light for fear that their deeds will be exposed. But whoever lives by the truth comes into the light, so that it may be seen plainly that what they have done has been done in the sight of God.

John 3:17-21

I Call Him By Name

Shoppet, one day I will have to stand before You and be held accountable for all that I have done. While that is a sobering thought, I pray that You draw me nearer today. I hunger for Your presence and to do right in Your eyes. My heart longs to please You, not only as my King but also as my Shoppet. Teach me to pass down Your compassion and justice to the children You've lent to me to raise. Thank You for Your faith in me to raise these precious babies. Thank You that You reign on Your throne today, tomorrow, and forevermore. Amen.

Frenemies

Have you ever been stabbed or shot in the back? Okay, maybe that's a bit extreme; maybe you can relate to a painful lip wax? This type of pain emerges in the aftermath of gossip. No joke. Proverbs 18:21 reads: "The tongue has the power of life or death, and those who love it will eat of its fruit." It's a sobering fact and something that dwells in my heart after a painful experience last year.

My husband and I lost several close friends, and it was one of the most miserable summers of my life (I'd rather have been pregnant with quadruplets in our hot humid Nebraska summers than go through that experience again). When a heart is wounded it goes to anyone to find comfort, and that usually means talking to several good friends, who then form opinions and pass them on to other good friends. Get the picture yet? Soon I heard about the gossip and because I had to have the last word, I made sure everyone knew my point of view and the gossip continued.

It became uncomfortable to go to church. A glance, smirk, or cold shoulder turned into Morse code in which my husband and I perceived that we were not wanted and unwelcome. The gossip had caused so much tension, we stepped down from service positions in the church. It was too much to be sitting at the table with these women and the big elephant in the room that no one wanted to point out or discuss. I then felt the need to go to Connie, the pastor's wife, and ask what she knew or heard about me. I needed to know she didn't judge me. After all, her opinion of me was very important, right?

Can you imagine how sick and half insane I was to go and approach the pastor's wife about the issue? Seriously, it took nearly a month for me to walk back into my church. Not because I was martyred and hated (that scenario would have been easier to deal with), it was because of my pride and what God revealed to me in the meeting. I wasn't the only guilty party, either. There was plenty of gossip, slander, and fact checking coming from the other gals too. Nevertheless, that's not the point. During the meeting, Connie had each of us read Scripture about slander and dissension and what thse do to our emotions. God took this opportunity to knock out the weak bricks and rebuild a new foundation on how to keep my mouth shut!

He used this moment to help each of us reflect on our actions, and how we contributed to judging and gossiping about each other. If I had a dollar for every woman who had a prayer request or concern about another woman, I'd be richer than the Rockefellers. God wants to bring to our attention that we should not use prayer requests, concerns, fact checking, and chitchat to talk about another sister in Christ. Call me crazy, but it does make sense. I felt that I had not gossiped about these women, my friends, but God revealed to me that unless we go directly to the woman in question with our concern, we are indeed gossiping.

When we gossip, we are feeling inadequate about ourselves. We think we need to knock another woman down a level. Once we begin comparing ourselves, the rivalry begins. It continues to snowball... more like an avalanche. If it gets out of control, it can crush an entire church. Christians often forget the church body isn't a building; it is made up of believers, each holding an essential part in the church itself. (Read 1 Corinthians 12:12-31.) Gossip causes wounded women and dissension in our church body. God alone is our judge. He makes it very clear that we have no place to pass judgment on anyone else. Matthew 7:1-5 sums it up nicely.

> *Do not judge, or you too will be judged. For in the same way you judge others, you will be judged, and with the measure you use, it will be measured to you. Why do you look at the speck of sawdust in your brother's eye and pay no attention to the plank in your own eye? How can you say to your brother, "Let me take the speck out of your eye," when all the time there is a plank in your own eye? You hypocrite, first take the plank out of your own eye, and then you will see clearly to remove the speck from your brother's eye.*

Now that no one is firing loaded tongues anymore, there is peace once again; but make no mistake, our relationships are not the same. Some for better, some for worse. One gal in particular takes offense at anything I say and do. It made me realize two things. One: God alone is our judge. Two: He alone is our defender and the only audience we should be concerned about. While I can't get her to like me, I can look to God, asking that my security and identity come from Him.

I pray that we, as women, become wiser to the abilities our tongues have in terms of power. It's a power that doesn't belong to us, but to our Judge. When God revealed that He alone is our Judge, He intended for us to strive towards the goals He set for us: His intention for our tongues was to build each other up in the body of Christ. Instead, when we cast judgment and voice it for all to hear, our focus is no longer what God calls us to do; instead, we are striving to prove the worthlessness of that rumor. Of all the lessons learned, these were by far the most painful. Practice wisdom with your words and remember that little ones are watching all you do.

Mama's Time-Out

- Recall a time when gossip wounded you. What did you do about it? The next time you are tempted to set a rumor straight or you are bitter about something someone said about you, get on your knees and take it to God. Then tactfully approach the person who made the statement, not the person who told you.

- God has given us ways to restore unity with one another, if there is an issue that needs to be resolved, seek out godly counsel. Ask that person to be the mediator between the one you are at odds with and you. Invite God into the meeting and ask Him for restoration.

Today's Love Note

Do not let any unwholesome talk come out of your mouths, but only what is helpful for building others up according to their needs, that it may benefit those who listen. And do not grieve the Holy Spirit of God, with whom you were sealed for the day of redemption. Get rid of all bitterness, rage and anger, brawling and slander, along with every form of malice. Be kind and compassionate to one another, forgiving each other, just as in Christ God forgave you.

Ephesians 4:29-32

I Call Him By Name

Shoppet, Your name means Judge. I come to You in heavy reverence that You are my Rock, my Healer, my Friend, but You are also my Judge. Quicken my heart so that I may remember that my tongue is for building others up. When I want to tear someone down, I pray to come to You first. I want to bring You my thoughts, my discouragement, and my bitterness. Thank You God that You alone are my Judge. Thank You that I only have to strive to please an audience of one. Shoppet, help me to set this example before my children so they may walk before You in freedom. Amen.

MIQWEH YISRAEL

The Lord Is Hope

Psalms 25:5; 39:7; Isaiah 40:31; Jeremiah 17:5-8; Hebrews 6:19; Titus 2:13

*"For everything that was written in the past was written to teach us,
so that through endurance and encouragement,
of the Scriptures, we might have hope."*

ROMANS 15:4

Hope Is Spelled
M-I-Q-W-E-H Y-I-S-R-A-E-L

An example of hope, though superficial, is when I tried to dye my hair a lighter shade of blond. We as women cling to the hope we can look younger than our age for just a little while longer with tricks like hair dye. While the dye was burning my scalp and bleaching my hair, I pampered myself with chocolates, fashion magazines and painting my daughter's toes. When the forty-five minutes were up to wash out the dye, I hopped into the shower knowing that I would look like the summer blond I was in high school. But when I got out and started drying my hair, I squealed at the color I saw in the mirror and had my hair stylist on speed dial. Before Amy could say a word she heard, "Amy! Amyyyyyyy! It's orange! My hair is orange! What am I gonna do? I have to go home in a couple of weeks to see my mother and you know what that's like." I cried into the phone as I attempted to not hyperventilate.

"Heather it's 10:38 at night. What do you want me to do about it now?"

"Amy, it's ORANGE! Do I need to spell it out for you?"

"Put Chris on the phone," Amy growled, wanting to make sure it was an emergency. Chris glanced at me and nonchalantly stated, "It's more like burnt yellow," and tossed the phone back, watching me curl up into a ball on our bed and pummel the pillows.

"Come in at 8:30 and don't be late! Tell your husband that the next time you want to dye your hair that it costs $120.00 for color corrections versus getting highlights!" Amy yelled into the phone before hanging up. The next morning I was there with my hair disaster, which Amy peered at stating, "It's not that bad, more like chicken yellow."

Not only did Amy restore my hair using dark low lights, but she also restored my hope in looking normal. It brought our relationship as friends onto a new playing field as she felt free to open up about her hopes of God bringing her a mate (funny how hair bonding moments do that). Amy had been hoping day in and day out, more than fourteen years, for God to bring her a husband. After hoping in the Lord's plans, she is now married, expecting their first child, and I still have awesome hair!

Hope is part of being a woman. We never stop hoping. We hope that the pregnancy test turns blue; we hope it's a boy, or we hope it's a girl. We then hope our twin girls stay in the bras we have because there are no bigger sizes for them to flow into. We hope our outie belly button will return to the innie it used to be instead of looking like a piece of cauliflower. We hope labor won't be as traumatic and painful as the last time, or we hope we get our epidural before due time. We hope we don't kill our husbands in the midst of the pain, and we hope our baby is healthy as we push her or him out, or in my case I really hoped I'd get to strangle my doctor and "epidural doctor" because I felt every bit of Tori's big debut, pushing through at ten pounds, two ounces.

We hope while we are in public that no screaming baby triggers the mystery of the milk reflex which often floods our shirts with perfect target stains around our breasts. We hope we will at least get three hours of sleep tonight, and we hope this stage ends soon. We hope the teenage years are better than the toddler years (the debate is still out as my daughter is entering the teen years while I deal with my terrible two Tori). We are fountains of hope. We live and breathe the word hope.

Hope fuels our hearts and our bodies with energy to get through "one of those days." Take for example my friend Adrienne. Her daughter Maya is nearly two, and she just found out she is having a baby . . . well babies—twins! She's been in shock for the last two weeks and is now adjusting to the idea of twice the work. She has hope that if God planned this, He can bring her through this or at least keep her sanity intact. (By the way, the twins are almost a year old. Adrienne has been the most confident and sane mother I've seen with twins.)

God's very nature brings us hope. The Hebrew word for hope is Miqweh.

The name of God that encompasses hope is Miqweh Yisrael which means the Hope of Israel (Larry Richards, *Encyclopedia of Bible Words*). This facet of God is shown time and again throughout Scriptures in the stories of Job, Esther, Joshua, and Jacob. When Jesus was sent to us, He became hope in human form. God becomes the God who saves His people; we can put our ultimate trust in Him. Miqweh Yisrael's definition encourages us to look ahead towards the future with confident expectation. As we focus our attention on Him, we find confidence in our situation. We find patience for the outcome. Take a look at the verses listed below, all are referenced from the Bible:

- Psalm 71:14 says, "But for me I will always hope; I will praise you more and more."
- Psalm 119: 49-50 says, "Remember your word to your servant, for you have given me hope. My comfort in my suffering is this: Your promise preserves my life."
- Psalm 130:5, 7 says, "I wait for the LORD, my whole being waits, and in his word I put my hope.... Israel, put your hope in the LORD, for with the LORD is unfailing love and with him is full redemption."
- Hebrews 6:19 says, "We have this hope as an anchor for the soul, firm and secure."

The writers who penned the Scriptures above had confidence in God about their futures. The more they waited and hoped in God, the more they wanted to praise Him. They knew that putting their hope in God meant trusting Him completely with their lives. When we have hope, we have courage because God affirms through His Word that He is trustworthy. Whatever situation you may be facing, a screaming child, going back to work, stressing about a bill, or dealing with antics of a rebellious tween, God is waiting for you to put your hope in Him. Give Him your troubles and praise Him as you talk to Him. He will give you trust, patience, and endurance to make it through.

Mama's Time-Out

- Have you put God in a box? Have you limited what you think God can do? If so, pray that God helps you with your views of Him and that He blows the lid off the box you placed Him in.
- What does it mean to trust people versus trusting and hoping in God?

🔸 Throughout each day, teach your children that their hope in Him is founded on a God who is trustworthy and they can be confident He has their best intentions in mind.

Today's Love Note

Therefore, since we have been justified through faith,
we have peace with God through our Lord Jesus Christ,
through whom we have gained access by faith into this
grace in which we now stand.
And we boast in the hope of the glory of God.
Not only so, but we also glory in our sufferings,
because we know that suffering produces perseverance;
perseverance, character; and character, hope.
And hope does not put us to shame, because God's love has been
poured out into our hearts through the Holy Spirit,
who has been given to us.

Romans 5:1-5

I Call Him By Name

You are the hope of Israel, Miqweh Yisrael. You are also my hope. No matter the situation, even if things look bleak, I can put my heart in Your hands. Open my heart to new depths of trust and hope in You. You are the one in whom I can place my ultimate trust. I can bring You my frustrations, my fears, and my worries because I know that when I place them on Your altar, joy in You wells up in my heart. Thank You for being the ultimate hope for us all. In Your Son's precious name, amen.

Here's Hoping

I have no business raising children (but I'm not in charge of my uterus either, so take it up with God). My thoughts are full of "what ifs" and worst-case scenarios. I often see what's on the news and then my imagination runs away with me as I begin to hyperventilate. I mean, what I just saw on the tube could possibly happen to my kids, right? I also wonder how a particular calamity will affect my children, like the oil spill. Is it going to cause a huge ecological shift and my babies will grow up wearing gas masks? Or how about the trillions of dollars of debt we have? I've imagined my children living in cardboard boxes because everything has been taxed to pay back the debt.

In these moments, I wonder how my daughter will survive with her ADD and Asperger's. (For more information about it, check out help4adhd.org. Or if you are curious about Asperger's, visit Autismspeaks.org.) She doesn't pick up on the social cues; she can't tell if someone is angry or sarcastic unless they're yelling at her. How will she blend in? Will anyone else notice she is different? My worries for her are whether or not she will get through middle school, let alone high school. What about college and getting a job? Will she be washing dishes the rest of her life because I didn't help her enough with her homework? Lord, help me tame the imagination please!

While going through the process of securing resources and additional help for Cheyenne in school, I was met with unexpected negativity over her diagnosis. It was the stereotypical "she is unruly, unloved, and undisciplined" reaction that I got from many well-meaning and snotty "my child is better than yours" parents. As hard as it was to control my reactions, I began to worry that maybe I didn't do enough for Cheyenne as an infant; after all, I was a teenager. Maybe putting her in daycare caused it, maybe it was being at a wild senior party that caused it, or maybe I didn't spend enough time with her as a baby that caused it.

Chy and I were devastated when her school placed her on academic probation for low grades. That meant that she had until the end of the semester to improve her overall school habits or she would have to go back to public school. Even then, the problems she was having would still follow her, leaving her back in the same situation of low grades, unable to focus on the task at hand, and messy work. We scrambled to get the evaluation process implemented as we raced against the clock to pull her grades up before the end of the semester. Each time she received her progress reports, I felt I was losing hope. Why isn't God helping her? Why aren't her teachers helping her more? What was the point in jumping through all these hoops if she was on the verge of getting kicked out?

Then we found the missing piece of the puzzle. It wasn't the teachers' faults or our own. We had known for quite some time about her diagnosis of Inattentive ADD, but we learned she also struggled with Asperger's. Cheyenne had struggled with school since the beginning and we wondered how else we could help her.

In first grade, she floundered because she couldn't see the words like everyone else. She had to learn a completely new way to read by memorizing the look of a word. In second grade, we found out she was nearly blind in one eye. It required glasses and sporting an eye patch all day, every day. In third, she was the little girl who the girls left out in their games, making themselves superior in her eyes. In fourth, we realized she couldn't focus and required different learning strategies with the diagnosis of Inattentive ADD. The missing piece of the puzzle of Cheyenne was Asperger's.

Middle school holds all new challenges, which Cheyenne has to fight through to make sense of the world. She wants to fit in, to look like everyone else, to be able to laugh at jokes and be silly like the rest of her peers. But Cheyenne doesn't get jokes. She has curly hair, glasses, and is taller than her teacher. In sixth grade, she is realizing her world is not like everyone else's. She has to fight the way her mind interprets all of its sensory miscommunications (imagine trying to have a conversation while standing in the middle of a casino with every machine hitting jackpot at once and confetti blowing everywhere). Everything from smells wafting in the air to the way her clothing feels on her body, she has to learn to tune out in order to process what is happening within the bounds of the socialization happening around her.

I was devastated over this new development, yet hopeful because we had an answer. It was as if God gave us the key to unlock the door to her learning abilities, to understand her world. We weren't bad parents, nor was she a bad kid. She was just growing up different.

Yet worry crept in with my other two kids. Would I be facing the same struggles with them when they entered school? What then? As I prayed, I heard God gently direct me to Psalm 139:13-16.

> *For you created my inmost being; you knit me together in my mother's womb. I praise you because I am fearfully and wonderfully made; your works are wonderful, I know full well my frame was not hidden from you when I was made in the secret place. When I was woven together in the depths of the earth, your eyes saw my unformed body. All the days ordained for me were written in your book before one of them came to be.*

God knew exactly what He was doing while Cheyenne was woven together within my womb. He knew what her personality would be like and He knew how she would learn. He created her to be artistic, bubbly, and full of life. He created her to love nature, and He created her to learn differently. He allowed her differences to bring Him glory. As He was whispering these words to me, hope trickled into my heart. Cheyenne wasn't made with a short circuit. He created her with this "disorder" as a part of who she is. When she does lock in on something that sparks her interest, she becomes a walking encyclopedia and reflects what she has learned in ways that amaze her teachers and her parents. It becomes her passion. This passion reflects her Maker and glorifies Him.

Though she struggles with focus and schoolwork, we know that she wasn't created to be the best student; God had another purpose in mind. The gifts, abilities and talents God did create in her will one day glorify Him beyond my wildest imagination. It may be a struggle to get through school, but there is hope. Hope in who she is learning to be, hope in what she will one day become, and hope in who she is now.

When you begin to question God, go to Him as Miqweh Yisrael and ask Him to fill you with insight and, of course, hope. It will remind you to look to the future while opening your eyes to His master plan. Trust in Him and there your hope will be renewed and strengthened.

Mama's Time-Out

- Do you have a child with a disability? In what ways do you struggle with hope? Do you bring your concerns to God?

- Having a child with a disability is at times heart-wrenching, but there are resources out there to help your child attain the best quality of life. Besides going to God with your concerns, contact your public school to find out about resources your community has to offer.

Today's Love Note

*Yet this I call to mind
and therefore I have hope:
Because of the LORD's great love we are not consumed,
for his compassions never fail.
They are new every morning;
great is your faithfulness.
I say to myself, "The LORD is my portion;
therefore I will wait for him."
The LORD is good to those whose hope is in him,
to the one who seeks him;
it is good to wait quietly
for the salvation of the LORD.*

Lamentations 3:21-26

I Call Him By Name

Father, today as I come to You, I pray that You restore my hope in You. You are the essence of hope and my reserves are dry. You know my struggles, my doubts, and my worries. I lay them at Your altar because You are more than capable of taking care of each concern. I pray that a river of hope flows forth as I learn to look to You as Miqweh Yisrael. In Your name I pray, amen.

MELEK

King of Kings

Zechariah 4:19; 1 Timothy 1:17; 6:15; Revelation 19:16

Now if we are children, then we are heirs—heirs of God and co-heirs with Christ, if indeed we share in his sufferings in order that we may also share in his glory.

Romans 8:17

Sounds Like an Onion to Me

As the news anchor switched to the next story, I burst into tears burdened with dread.

"How could I be so stupid?" I wondered aloud as Chris walked in the door.

"Why are you crying now?" he asked bewildered once again by his pregnant and emotional wife.

"What were we thinking? We can't bring a child into this horrible world! There was another rape and murder on the news here in town. We were selfish to do this!" I sobbed. Emotions and hormones bubbled to the surface, threatening to spill over like tidal waves as I wondered how I would protect my baby. Wanting the best for my unborn child overwhelmed me each day as I watched the news. Rapes, robberies, and murders are as common as weeds in the front yard. No matter where I turned, there were awful stories that made me question if there is any way to keep my child in utero as long as possible.

"Babe, that's just the way life is. You gotta stop watching that stuff," he said as he walked over and turned off our ancient TV. Of course his "helpful" words only aggravated the situation causing the closest magazine to be chucked at his head while I attempted to storm my way to the bedroom (it was more like heavy waddling).

If God is truly King, then why is the world so messed up? Why are there children starving on our streets, why do we have Amber Alerts? Why do teachers have to go through background checks, and why do we have women selling themselves on the streets and human trafficking? Why do we have overcrowded prisons full of people who are evil? If God is King, why is all of this allowed? Why isn't He doing something about it? Most of all, what was I thinking to bring a child into this world? My goodness I must be insane.

Let's face it. We are nuts to bring children into this fallen world. The world doesn't belong to us. It belongs to God, but in the meantime, His adversary is inflicting devastation in as many lives as possible to keep us from experiencing and knowing God. What better way to prevent a "could be" Christian than by causing horror and evil? Many life events and circumstances are so tragic that they can wound a soul for a lifetime causing people to become embittered towards God. Yet all of us know deep down that we have a Maker, we have a God who is King of kings.

When life's events "happen" to us, we turn to God and say, "Why didn't You do something about it? Why didn't You prevent it?" After facing some unspeakable horrors myself, I've walked out on the other side, hand in hand with Jesus. I've learned that people aren't evil, nor is this world evil; instead, there are two reasons we seem to miss when faced with hurt and pain. One is that the enemy knows he has very little time left here on this earth, so he is on the prowl to kill, steal, and destroy God's beloved people. Two, God is biding time with His plan. God already took care of the problem 2000 years ago when His Son was nailed to that cross. Every choice, every mistake, and every evil was laid on Christ so that we can have a choice. We can choose to love God and honor Him as King or choose life without Him. While the rest of the world chooses to live in the moment and commit unspeakable acts, know that Jesus was whipped, stripped, and bloodied for us. From the littlest white lie to murder. It was all laid on Him.

The New Testament speaks of Jesus as being King of kings because His perfect obedience to do the will of His Father ushered in a new age where we have the choice to love God or turn away, an age where one day we all will rule with Jesus as King. When that day happens, there will be no more tears or pain. As disturbing as it sounds, a child will be able to play in the midst of a cobra den and there will be no fear. There will be complete peace and joy. Isaiah 11:6-9 reads:

> *The wolf will live with the lamb, the leopard will lie down with the goat, the calf and the lion and the yearling together; and a little child shall lead them. The cow will feed with the bear, their young will lie down together, and the lion will eat straw like the ox. The*

infant will play near the hole of the cobra, and the young child put his hand into the viper's nest. They will neither harm nor destroy on my holy mountain, for the earth will be full of the knowledge of the Lord, *as the waters cover the sea.*

Yahweh Melek may sound like a cousin to our flavorful green onions that we dice and throw on salads, but it's God's Hebrew name as King. Saul was the first king of God's people, followed by King David, who was legendary as a man after God's own heart. In those days, calamities struck the nations as people strayed from God. Habakkuk is one of the best books of the Bible to reference when we wonder why God allows evil and injustice on His people.

Habakkuk questioned why God allowed the Babylonians to rise up and destroy God's people. He wondered why God would allow a ruthless and evil nation to rise up over God's people and questioned God's rule and holiness. God responded that the righteous should be faithful and wait on Him. Instead of continuing to question God, Habakkuk turned around and praised Him. This is the example we are to follow. Though wickedness may reign and disaster strikes God's loved ones in this day and age, we are not to question God. Instead, we are to praise God and teach our children that God is still the Ruler and will one day usher in His new kingdom. As much as it sounds like a fairy tale, this is what we are to teach our children. We teach them to wait, be patient, and praise the God who has a plan.

Yahweh Melek did something that even left the angels awestruck. He gave us free will. It sets us apart from every other living creature. Being human, with free will, and a woman is a wondrous thing (although potentially dangerous when we have extra hormones coursing through our body once a month). We have the choice to choose to fall in love with God or walk away.

Looking at our King as a parent, He could prevent evil from happening but if He did, it would take away our free will. We would be robots, never experiencing the triumph and glory of His ultimate design. Instead of making us choose to do right, we would have no choice. God would have to supernaturally intervene 100 percent of the time. Much like when we give our children choices, like cleaning their rooms or studying for their spelling tests, if they make the choice to not do it, we would have to intervene by doing it for them. I don't know about you, but that sounds like a recipe for having my children live with me for the rest of their lives. Instead of raising successful, sharp-minded people, it would make them incapable of making any choice. I'd much rather have my 40s and 50s spent in freedom to enjoy watching my children succeed by making the right choices.

The other option would be for God to remove everyone who commits evil acts. As entertaining as it sounds to have God smite those who commit evil—there would be no one left. All sin is evil. Sin means to miss the mark, and God has never missed the mark; He is holy and set apart. As for me, I miss it on a daily basis with not-so-nice thoughts, pride, and sometimes selfishness. In God's eyes, a tiny white lie is just as evil as murder. God is concerned about the evil in this world. The Old Testament proves His concern after He handed down laws and commandments to Moses. Then because God knew that it wouldn't be enough, His own Son was sacrificed to give us the choice to follow God and to give more time for all of us to make the choice to follow Him.

When my children come to me and ask why God allows bad things to happen, I creatively lead them back to God's Word while teaching them what it says. Romans 3:23, Ecclesiastes 7:20, 1 John 1:8, Romans 5:12, 2 Peter 3:9 are the sources I use when they ask these questions. Sometimes there are no explanations for the wrongs in this world. I didn't realize my daughter Chy was within earshot of the news. As I was in the bedroom folding the millionth load of laundry, the news turned to a story our state was following. The details were horrific. A two-year-old little girl was beaten to death by her father with a belt for wetting the bed. Chy came into the room crying, asking why it had to happen. I had no answer. Instead we prayed that her father might come to know Jesus in prison. We prayed God would protect other little girls from that kind of harm. And we prayed He would give us a voice and courage for other little girls.

As hard as it is, we cannot shut out the world. Nor can we shelter our children from what is happening. Instead, we can show them how to rely on Jesus. Teaching them justice and vengeance belong to our King. We can be the bridge to their hearts, showing them how to pray for God's people, creating compassion. I also remind them that God does promise severe consequences to those who commit evil acts on the innocent. Justice and vengeance are in His hands alone. Nothing causes God's anger more than when the innocent are harmed. His consequences of evil and sin are much worse than we could ever imagine. Justice and vengeance are in His hands alone.

Our time is running short and He has drawn a line in the sand. God will judge and rule over all. One day there will be joy, happiness, peace, and a perfect world to live in. In the meantime, we are to pray that God's kingdom comes soon.

Mama's Time-Out

How do you teach your children about God as Ruler over all? When they ask questions like why does God allow bad things to happen to good people, what is your response?

Today's Love Note

*Endow the king with your justice, O God, the royal son with your righteousness.
May he judge your people in righteousness, your afflicted ones with justice.
May the mountains bring prosperity to the people,
the hills the fruit of righteousness.
May he defend the afflicted among the people and save
the children of the needy; may he crush the oppressor.
May he endure as long as the sun, as long as the moon, through all generations.
May he be like rain falling on a mown field, like showers watering the earth.
In his days may the righteous flourish and
prosperity abound till the moon is no more.
May he rule from sea to sea and from the River to the ends of the earth.*

Psalm 72:1-8

I Call Him By Name

Father God, I acknowledge You as King of kings. Your mighty name as Yahweh Melek says it all. It says You are holy, You are sovereign, You are just. Thank You for Your rule and leadership. Though the earth is filled with pain and sin, I know that You have a plan and I know that I am in Your hands. Help me to not question why evil happens but help me to praise You. Help me to pray for mercy, compassion, and courage for Your people as well as my kids. Thank You for Your love and leadership and I pray that Your will be done on this earth. Usher in Your kingdom God. Come soon. Amen.

Modern-Day Princess

Apparently my youngest thinks she is the ruler of the household. She will run through the house with her hands on her hips, stop with her feet spread apart, and point a finger at her brother, saying, "You stop now, I say so!" with as much regalness as she can muster. If Elijah ignores her command, she will grab his face in both of her hands, scrunch up her face, and say, "I princess, you obey." This usually ends up with Elijah making Tori face plant on the floor, but she's not down for long. She cries for Mommy and tells me of her latest plight as I pick her up, dusting off her ruffled blue princess dress. Being quick to diffuse any more potential disloyal subjects, I quickly hand my little princess a monster truck and she dances off to the kitchen to play. I am astonished by her self-esteem and view of the world. If only I could muster as much faith in who I am in Christ as she does, I wouldn't have nearly as many "issues" to deal with.

My daughters have been told since they were born that they are loved, they are princesses. Lately they have been taught they are real-life princesses because God adopted them into His family when they gave their hearts to Jesus. Both Cheyenne and Tori have been honored as princesses through our love for them and through several events at our church. They have been given the opportunity to be crowned and honored as God's chosen ones.

When I first entered into God's family a few years ago, I was tickled and exhilarated by a pink T-shirt I discovered at our local Christian bookstore.

On the front it said "Genuine Princess," while the back read, "My Daddy is the King of Kings." The thought astounded me. A girl who's been soiled, dirtied, broken, and thrown to the curb was actually royalty. The very idea at first was hard to accept. How could someone like me who's lived a life of sin, was used, abused, and forsaken be loved and considered royalty? It may seem like an easy concept for those of you who have lived as children of God from a young age, but for someone who has been tossed aside and broken like myself, it's too much to accept, to understand.

Think for a moment that you are a child. Your parents loved you and called you their little princess while the love of Christ flowed through your parents to you. As you grew up, your parents taught you the very nature of God while endowing you with His love and sacrifice. They also taught you that you were an heir to His kingdom when you accepted Christ into your heart. For someone like me whose life was filled with pain, regret, and poor choices, it's humbling enough knowing God pardoned my transgressions, but the idea of royalty takes it to a whole new level.

Every day my daughters love to dress up in their princess dresses, crowns, and shoes (my oldest steals my prom dresses). They prance through the house with an air of dignity, as if to say, "I'm a princess and I am so loved." They giggle and their hearts are filled with joy as their Dad and I agree they are princesses, real-life princesses. As they watch movies like "Cinderella" and "Beauty and the Beast," they have no problem believing that they are like those characters. Life may throw them a curve ball, like parents dying or being captured by an evil emissary. But at the end of the movie, my girls rejoice because they know their real prince, Jesus, will one day come and usher them into God's kingdom where they will forever live as princesses of God.

My daughters know they are loved and are royalty; it's certainly a different reflection I see in the eyes of the teen girls I serve through Teen MOPS (Mothers of Preschoolers). Their eyes reflect brokenness, the pain of being unloved, and innocence lost. Every Tuesday I take a moment to pray so that I can allow Christ to use me to pour His love and truths into these girls. I tell them several things:

- They are fully accepted by God and me no matter what anyone says.
- They are worth more than gold.
- God created them for His purpose.
- God created them in beauty.

- No matter what they have done or said, they belong to God and are still special to God.
- They are precious in Jesus' eyes.
- Nothing they have done or ever will do can make them less in His eyes.
- They are loved, honored, and treasured by Jesus no matter the past, present, or future.

These truths are taught to my Teen MOPS moms, and they also apply to you. No matter the past, God still loves you. No matter your situation or what you've done, God still cares for you. If you or your daughters struggle with self-esteem and accepting that God loves you in this capacity, read the book of Esther, and follow up with the devotional, *For a Time Such as This* by Lisa Ryan, or *Raising Up Girls* by Dr. James Dobson.

Our media teaches us there is no such thing as a modern-day princess; instead, we need to ponytail our hair and make the impossible happen. Our self-esteem is based on our performance, beauty, age, and how sensual we can be. I thought the same way for years before I came to God and He taught me what a real princess looks like. Real princesses don't have good self esteem, they have God-esteem. This esteem comes from creating a foundation on who we are in Him. Forget what the world says; it's view of royalty and beauty is distorted. So how does God see you?

Ephesians 2:10 says, "For we are God's handiwork, created in Christ Jesus to do good works, which God prepared in advance for us to do."

First Peter 3:3-4 says, "Your beauty should not come from outward adornment, such as elaborate hairstyles and the wearing of gold jewelry or fine clothes. Rather, it should be that of your inner self, the unfading beauty of a gentle and quiet spirit, which is of great worth in God's sight."

This last Scripture is often misinterpreted. Some who read it think that a woman is of great worth if she is silent and plain. That's not what God planned for His princesses. Instead, God wants us to know that we are to find our beauty from spending time with Him. Our self-esteem isn't based on the finest of clothes and the latest fashion, it's based on knowing who we are in Him. Now how do you like those apples? The next time a beauty commercial or celebrity trend is making you feel inferior, go to God and soak in His presence, He will tell you who you really are.

God has reminded me through His love and grace that I am His princess. It doesn't matter what someone has done to me or what has happened in my past. I am still an heir to His kingdom. I am reminded to see the good in what God created in me.

One day each of us will enter the gates of God's new kingdom. Jesus will be there waiting to greet us and hug His special princesses. He will then take away our soiled and tattered garments while clothing us in the most beautiful gowns we could possibly imagine. Then He will announce to the rest of the kingdom our names and our royal title has His princesses: "Behold, this one, this woman child is mine!" In the meantime, I will dream of the day my Prince will come as I fold laundry and care for the princesses in my charge.

Mama's Time-Out

- In order to teach your child that she is a real princess, pick up the book *God's little Princess Devotional Bible Story Book* by Sheila Walsh. Or may I suggest a fun-filled afternoon making crowns out of foil and teaching your princess the Scripture that refers to her as an heir to God's throne.

- Gaining more insight to your little girl as she is growing up is a great way to stay connected with her and gain more patience with her. Pick up a copy of Dr. James Dobson's book, *Raising Up Girls*. It's been a valuable resource for both my girls.

Today's Love Note

You are all sons [daughters] of God through faith in Christ Jesus, for all of you who were baptized into Christ have clothed yourselves with Christ. There is neither Jew nor Greek, slave nor free, male nor female, for you are all one in Christ Jesus.
If you belong to Christ, then you are Abraham's seed, and heirs according to the promise.

Galatians 3:27-29

I Call Him By Name

My King, through Your love and great compassion, You created me for Your kingdom. You alone are the King of kings. You alone are ruler of all. Too wonderful is the thought that I belong to You, that one day I will rule with You. You are my King and I am a co-heir because of Your Son Jesus. Thank You for this revelation. Help me to live as Your daughter. Guide me as I parent Your princesses and princes in my charge. Thank You Father, thank You O King! You will rule forever and ever. Amen.

YAHWEH TSURI

The Lord Is My Rock

2 Samuel 22:2-4; Psalm 125:1-2; 1 Corinthians 10:1-5

For in Scripture it says:
"See, I lay a stone in Zion,
a chosen and precious cornerstone,
and the one who trusts in him
will never be put to shame."

1 Peter 2:6

In His Hands

"We will, we will ROCK YOU. Oh ya, we will, we will ROCK YOU," Elijah chanted as he stomped through the house with his cars and soccer ball, while I lay on the couch sick as a dog to my stomach, drooling on my pillow. He just learned the song after watching soccer on TV with Daddy. The timing was impeccable because I had a migraine. Need I say more?

"You're rockin' it alright," I moaned, "but could you please whisper it and not stomp, pretty please?"

To which Lige replies, "Mommy that's not the point, I gotta be loud. It's what boys do!" he frankly lisped before parading through the house with his song.

"Lord, You're my rock, and my health and head are in Your hands. Please make this go away," I whispered.

That day, God chose to heal me through means of a shot in the rear at the clinic. Note to readers: When you get a migraine and you decide to go into the clinic for help, be sure you are wearing proper underwear; otherwise there will be embarrassment to heal from as well. I just thought I would mention that. Exposing my rear gave me no comfort, but knowing that I was in God's hands did. What better comfort can we give ourselves than when we involve our mighty God? He is best described as "the Rock." Rocks provide shelter, safety, and best of all, they are unmovable. They are unshakable. First Samuel 2:2 sums it up perfectly, "There is no Rock like our God."

The Hebrew word for God as our rock is Yahweh Tsuri and comes from three different Hebrew words, *sur, sela,* and *petra. Petra* is found mainly in the New Testament and symbolizes God as stability and safety. (It's also what Chris really wanted to name Tori. Can you imagine?) *Sela* means cliff of cleft of a mountain in which, in the Old Testament, people would go to for protection. *Sur* is the most common Hebrew reference to God as our rock, a mountain that was unshakable.

These can be found in several Scriptures: Psalm 62:1-2, Psalm 71:3, and Matthew 16:16. Through all the trials God's people faced, they saw Him as a strong foundation on which to stand. When Jesus came to earth, He became the spiritual foundation, the cornerstone of life in the spirit. He also became the stone that leaders and people rejected, and the cornerstone on which our churches build today (Larry Richards, *Encyclopedia of Bible Words*).

In this day and age, as moms we are pulled thousands of different directions either due to commitments or circumstances. Where do you turn when your marriage fails? Who do you cry out to when your child is hurt? Who do you call upon when dread fills your heart? Whom do you pray to in the everyday busyness of life that slaps you in the face? Is it the unshakeable God whose foundation has held firm since before the first dawn? When it feels like I'm in the spin cycle of life, I cling to Jesus like a wet rag. He is my anchor. The world attempts to toss us about and God's Word is the anchor that holds fast to our souls. Second Samuel 22:3 is one Scripture which I have memorized and recall when life gets overwhelming,

> *My God is my rock, in whom I take refuge, my shield and the horn of my salvation. He is my stronghold, my refuge and my savior--from violent men you save me.*

Even with something as simple as a migraine, I go to God. He cares about the smallest things in life. He cares about what you care about. If it's bothering you, rest assured that it bothers God, too. He wants you to stand on His foundation in the small stuff as well. I've had the best conversations with God during the wild school mornings that weigh me down and make me feel like an incapable mother. When we wake up late, Tori takes off her poopy diaper, and Cheyenne can't find her school uniform, I lift it all up to God because the enemy is there whispering in my ears how lame I am that I can't keep it together. Keeping my feet firm and steady on God's Word when the spin cycle is on keeps me from being shaken. He reminds me that every mama has mornings like these.

Rest assured on the days that you know you shouldn't have gotten out of bed, God is there. In the moments when news overwhelms you, He is there. He is there during the moments your child is throwing his greatest tantrum in the middle of your local supermarket. When life expects you to wear a new pair of heels that you aren't sure you're ready to navigate, God is steady, ready, and waiting. Hold firm to the foundation of Christ. Let Him be your cornerstone. Let Him build His home within you, and you'll be able to breathe "amen."

Mama's Time-Out

As a reminder that the Lord is your rock, find a smooth stone, palm sized; then take a marker and write the words, "The Lord is My Rock" on it. Find several if you'd like. Once you've written on them, place them in a glass jar where you can see them or scatter them all over your front porch. This will be a daily reminder to you how mighty your God is. It will be a comfort to see on the days that it seems as if everything is falling apart. I keep one in my purse, too.

Today's Love Note

*Those who trust in the LORD are like Mount Zion,
which cannot be shaken but endures forever.
As the mountains surround Jerusalem,
so the LORD surrounds his people
both now and forevermore.*

Psalm 125:1-2

I Call Him By Name

Yaweh Tsuri says so much about who You are. You are the Rock of ages, the foundation of our lives. You are reliable, capable, and unmovable. You are the same yesterday as You are today. Lord, when my days are spinning out of control, help me to look to You as my sure foundation which does not move nor ever change. When circumstances cause me to grow weary, train my eyes to look to You for comfort while grounding my feet to Your sure foundation. Thank You for revealing Your name to me and steadying my path. In Your beloved Son's name I pray. Amen.

Heart Is Where the Home Is

My favorite story of my daughter Cheyenne was at the tender age of two. She asked her Daddy about Jesus. At the time, both of us were searching for that missing piece of the puzzle in our lives. We both were in desperate need of God breathing His life into us, not to mention needing something steady to stand on. The conversation went like this:

"Daddy, do you believe in Jesus?" Cheyenne asked from the backseat on her way home from daycare.

"I guess so," Daddy replied.

"Do you know where He lives?" she asked as she played with her seat buckles.

"Well, in heaven. It's in the sky," Chris replied after a few moments.

"No He doesn't. He lives in your heart and He talks to me all the time."

"Ya, well He lives in heaven too, I heard," Daddy said pulling onto the highway.

"Daddy, can you see Him? Can you hear Him because He's talking to me right now. Look, He's sitting right next to me!" Cheyenne replied seriously. Chris was so unnerved that he craned his neck over the backseat just to be sure that no stranger was in the car and he drove off the road and into the ditch!

It was two years later that I gave my heart to Christ. Two full years later, my husband did the same. Since then we have poured over our Bibles, filling our lives and hearts with His Word. To this day Chris still feels his pulse race when he tells that story because of how very real Jesus was to our daughter.

He has become the very foundation we build on. When we moved into our new home, we went through the house praying, dedicating every room to God. We wanted His Word to live in our home. However, because I am a mother with a very active imagination, I tend to worry. I worry because I know the paths that lead away from God and I'm so fearful of my kids walking away from Him. At this point I would prefer to leave my children locked in their rooms until the age of thirty so we can surpass the rebellious teen years and the college years of freedom. That way I can ensure that my children will remain in Jesus and not in jail (or being a menace to society for that matter). While imagining these scenarios, God's Spirit whispers ever so loudly to mine (okay, it's more like yelling because we've had this conversation several times):

> *Therefore everyone who hears these words of mine and puts them into practice is like a wise man who built his house on the rock. The rain came down, the streams rose, and the winds blew and beat against that house; yet it did not fall, because it had its foundation on the rock. (Matthew 7:23-25)*

In essence, God is telling me that if I build my home on His foundation, I have nothing to worry about, even my children's free will. They may dabble in things as prodigal children but they will return to God, I have that hope. This Scripture reminds me of God's faithfulness, His permanence and protection. It reminds me that He is reliable and will give my children the choice to come to Him if they ever stray. This Scripture is also very important for moms. It shows the importance of our roles as mamas.

Remember the saying, "Home is where the heart is"? Where is your heart? Is it hidden with God's? Does it reflect what God is teaching you? If so, how is it reflected in your home? In the profession of mothering your children, your heart reflects the world, right from wrong, manners, pride, and who God is. Behind the front door of your home, you have become the foundation in which your child will relate to the world. As daunting as it sounds, you are their manual to life itself. With what you teach them, they will navigate life beyond your front porch.

When I first had this thought, I of course panicked because I am not a role model. I yell, whine, complain, and at times I am lazy. There are days when I don't so much as lift a finger; I lay on the floor playing with my kids while eating an entire bag of M & Ms (the one-pound bag, not the little ones). During my lazy days, and even on the days when I'm ready to turn in my two-weeks' notice (not sure who I'd give it to), I am reminded that my heart is the foundation of this home.

The cornerstone on which I build is Christ. The tools He has given me are all in His book. The structure, discipline, correction, and love are from what Jesus has given me. Christ was also the cornerstone for you and everyone else. King Josiah is a good example of this. Josiah became king at the age of eight after his grandfather Manasseh had ruled Judah over five decades and was one of the worst kings of all time. Manasseh not only blatantly ignored God and His laws, he also destroyed the temple, murdered priests, sacrificed one of his sons to a pagan god, and built pagan altars using pieces of the temple. When Josiah was sixteen, he wanted the temple rebuilt and, during this process, his scribes found an ancient text of God's laws. The wondrous part about it was that he likely found this scroll in the cornerstone of the temple, where it had been laid 300 years earlier! It was very common and symbolic in those days to place scrolls of importance into the cornerstones of buildings. The symbolism reflects what the prophets and Christ Himself said:

- "For in Scripture it says: 'See, I lay a stone in Zion, a chosen and precious cornerstone, and the one who trusts in him will never be put to shame'" (1 Peter 2:6).
- "So this is what the Sovereign LORD says: 'See, I lay a stone in Zion, a tested stone, a precious cornerstone for a sure foundation; the one who trusts will never be dismayed'" (Isaiah 28:16).
- "Built on the foundation of the apostles and prophets, with Christ Jesus himself as the chief cornerstone" (Ephesians 2:20).

Our hearts are the center of our homes. Christ is the center of our hearts; on Him we build the very foundation of life. Our example leads our children, even when you don't think they are paying attention or they are ignoring your example. Believe me when I say they are soaking it all up like a sponge. So with those thoughts I will leave you to decide to lead as best you can with God's grace to build on His foundation. Or you could just lock your children in their rooms until they're thirty.

Mama's Time-Out

Grab those mundane moments and turn them into memorable teaching moments. While running errands, pray out loud to Jesus, thanking Him for the warm weather, the color pink, or the shape of your child's nose.

- You can also use these moments to commit Christ to their memory banks in the form of songs. Check out www.gofishguys.com. It has God's principles with great music that won't drive you insane!

Today's Love Note

*Therefore everyone who hears these words of mine and puts them into practice is like a wise man who built his house on the rock.
The rain came down, the streams rose, and the winds blew and beat against that house; yet it did not fall, because it had its foundation on the rock.*
Matthew 7:24-25

I Call Him By Name

Father God, You are the light to my soul. I'm ever so thankful that You ignited a flame in my child's heart. There are so many days when I wonder if mothering is worth it, but Lord, You know how important my job is. Direct my thoughts, guide my words, and help me to pause when I am in the middle of building to be sure my foundation is built on You and what Jesus did for me. Jesus, You are the living stone, You are the temple that resides in my heart. Protect it, guide it, lead me and my children into the way everlasting. Pour Your strength into my heart. Thank You, Father God, Amen.

ABBA

Father, Daddy

Mark 14:36; Romans 8:14-16; 2 Corinthians 6:18; Galatians 4:6

Though my father and mother forsake me, the Lord will receive me.

Psalm 27:10

The Father

"Mommy, when will Daddy be back from working on that blue crane?" Elijah asked as he rubbed my face and smooched my hand.

"He will be gone for at least a week. He's taking three airplanes and a train to get to the Ukraine, Buddy." After a few moments to digest that information, Elijah says, "Mom that must be a really big crane. He needs to come home soon." I rubbed his head and decided not to explain again that Daddy wasn't going to work on a blue crane, but he was going to the Ukraine to close a business deal.

My kids love their daddy. The house is in a frenzy of anticipation at 5:00 p.m. every day. That's when Chris rolls down our street in his big red truck. The children can single out the sound of his engine over the rest of the trucks. Their eyes sparkle while their bodies dance in excitement when Daddy strolls up to the house. Chris is their best friend. He is primarily the one who takes them on the most exciting adventures like crawdad hunting, fishing, climbing on the roof to clean out the gutters, or working on projects in the garage.

Chris loves his children and sees to it each of their needs are met, ensuring the kids know they are loved and wanted. Each child has a precious and unique bond with daddy. With Cheyenne, Chris is patient and her confidant. With Elijah, he is his personal jungle gym and example of the male species. With Tori, he reassures her that she is the little princess. Chris loves his children the way God intended for us to love our children, and God loves us in the same manner as

Chris loves our kids. Jesus started a trend when He referred to God as His Father and that we as His children should do the same.

Prior to Jesus arriving on the scene and shaking things up, God was known as our creator (Elohim) and later Yahweh. Jesus taught us that we ought to pray to God as our Father. Jesus was breaking ground in how God viewed His people. Abba means father or more specifically "Daddy." A father is the head of the household and commands the most respect.

Our earthly daddies give us just a taste of what God is like. God is diplomatic, just, and sovereign in the throne room, but behind closed doors He invites us to snuggle in His lap. He is the one who disciplines and provides for all needs. He has the ultimate authority, but fathers have a softer side, which draws in children. This teaches the ultimate love our fathers have for our children, just as Abba Father does for us. Abba is found about 275 times in the New Testament (Larry Richards, *Every Name of God in the Bible*). This title suggests the intimacy of the relationship God wants to have with each of us. Just as Chris adores each of his children, so does God adore each of us.

One of the best portrayals of Christ's love is the parable Jesus told of the prodigal son in the book of Luke.

> *But while he was still a long way off, his father saw him and was filled with compassion for him; he ran to his son, threw his arms around him and kissed him.*
>
> *The son said to him, "Father, I have sinned against heaven and against you. I am no longer worthy to be called your son."*
>
> *But the father said to his servants, "Quick! Bring the best robe and put it on him. Put a ring on his finger and sandals on his feet. Bring the fattened calf and kill it. Let's have a feast and celebrate. For this son of mine was dead and is alive again; he was lost and is found." So they began to celebrate. (Luke 15:20-24)*

In Luke 15 we read about a farmer's son who disowns his father, demands his inheritance and parties until the money tree is picked bare. This naughty son sold himself into slavery to feed pigs, one of the most detestable jobs according to the Jewish people. While watching the pigs eat, he mustered the courage to return to his father's house as a servant, if nothing else, in order that he would have his basic needs provided for. The most breathtaking part of this story was the father's response. The father saw his son from a distance and began running to embrace his pig-smelling wayward son. In those days, elders were dignified. They did not lift up their cloaks, nor did they ever run. The way they carried themselves was symbolic of their status in society.

Let's dissect this dramatic scene a little more so you can understand how much God emulates the title of Father. In the parable, the father represents God and the wayward son is a sinner like you and me. Even though the son rejected his father, squandered the gifts bestowed on him, and lived in filth, the father broke every rule and custom to embrace his son, welcoming him home! The father didn't even ask about the money or what his son had done; instead, he told his servants to get the party started; only the best of the best would do, of course. He wanted to celebrate his son's return. He then dressed him in clean clothes, which also represents what Jesus did for us. Though we are sinners and we miss the mark on a daily basis, Christ's blood covers our sins. His sacrifice covers every mistake we make, including yesterday, today, and tomorrow.

You may have had a great example of a father's love through your Dad, or you may be like me and your father was nonexistent in childhood. Your earthly father may have sinned against you or harmed you in some way. Either way, your father's example still falls short of the amazing love your Father God has for you. It grieves my heart to know that some of you are heartbroken over the relationship you've had with your dad.

However, Jesus wants to introduce you to the heavenly Father. Jesus Himself committed His life and death on the cross so that we would know the undying and passionate love God has for us. Abba Father wants you to know Him. He wants an intimate relationship with you. The God of the universe doesn't care what mistakes we've made, whether or not we've walked away from Him and lived with the pigs. He doesn't care about where we have been or what we have done. He wants us to know how deep, how wide, and how infinite His love is for you and me. As our heavenly Father, He wants us to understand that His forgiveness and love are incomparable to anything we have ever known. Out of all the names and characteristics God has, He wants to be known as your Abba, your Daddy.

Our God wants to be intimately known as your Daddy. In your own words, pray to God and describe what you want to receive in your relationship with God as your Father. We have direct access to the throne through Jesus who is ready to present your requests and heart to God. If your heart has been broken because of the example of your earthly father, ask God to renew and repair your heart. Ask Him to open the gates of heaven and flood you with His example.

Mama's Time-Out

Honor your husband. Let him know how much it means to you and your children that he loves all of you. I've honored my husband with his favorite cake, and even did one of his chores on his "honey-do list."

Today's Love Note

*For those who are led by the Spirit of God are the children of God.
The Spirit you received does not make you slaves,
so that you live in fear again; rather, the Spirit you received
brought about your adoption to sonship. And by him we cry, "Abba, Father."
The Spirit himself testifies with our spirit that we are God's children.
Now if we are children, then we are heirs—heirs of God
and co-heirs with Christ, if indeed we share in his
sufferings in order that we may also share in his glory.*

Romans 8:14-17

I Call Him By Name

Father God, You alone are the greatest example of fatherly love. I pray that You will break the chains that enslave my heart. I pray that You will open the doors so that I may know You so much more as my heavenly Father. Abba, Father, I cry out to know You. I cry out so that You may hear my voice and come running. Open my eyes to the love You have for me. Thank You for sending Your Son to act on my behalf. It warms my heart to know that I am Your child and You are my Father. In Your name I pray. Amen.

Daddy

"Mommy, what's that paper you got there?" Elijah inquired as I was tucking Daddy's paystub away in our bill folder.

"It's Daddy's paycheck he gets for all the hard work he does, Babe," I replied as I organized the stack of bills.

"Oh. His job must be more special than yours because you don't get one of those," Elijah stated in his matter-of-fact way, while I suppressed the urge to growl and wondered who I could turn in my two weeks' notice to.

My kids have this uncanny ability to drive me up the wall with some of their points of view and comments. At the same time, I was glad my five-year-old son could appreciate the value of hard work; at least I hoped he did. Yet it reminded me of how our Father God worked His glory in a way that we could be free of death and sin. And for that I'm ever so thankful.

I know God most intimately as my Daddy because of the absence of my own father growing up. God has been my protector, provider, healer, comforter, cheerleader, and my least favorite, disciplinarian. Without God acting in these roles over the course of my life, I would never have developed into the healthy woman I am today (at times this is debatable). Perhaps one of the most innovative roles God has taken in my life is to answer prayers. By answering prayers, He has become the "yes man." Taking the lead from Jesus when He taught the disciples how to pray in Matthew 6:9-14:

> *This, then, is how you should pray:*
> *"Our Father in heaven,*
> *hallowed be your name,*
> *your kingdom come,*
> *your will be done,*
> *on earth as it is in heaven.*
> *Give us today our daily bread.*
> *And forgive us our debts,*
> *as we also have forgiven our debtors.*
> *And lead us not into temptation,*
> *but deliver us from the evil one."*

I learned to pray to my Father in heaven. From this Scripture I learned to pray God's will over my life. I learned to pray for the moment, and I also learned the hard lesson of forgiveness. One of the greatest blessings I've received in praying in this manner is the restoration of my family, my dreams, and watching my family members accept Christ one by one.

One of the colossal insights we have of God is that He wants to say yes to us, just as Daddies here on this earth love to say yes to their children. They love to watch their children's faces glow with joy and their hearts become lighter when Daddy says yes to their requests. God did just that for me. Since I've been adopted into God's family, my deepest desire was for God to shake my father to his senses. I wanted so badly to be a "Daddy's girl," and I wanted so badly for my Dad to be free of the bondage he was in. Since my father was 14, he has been an alcoholic and drug addict. Try as they might, my grandparents couldn't free my dad from the chains he was in, nor did losing his children and wife. I'm sure many of you reading this understand the grief that captured my heart over the life I was subjected to because of my father's issues.

God does say yes; He does answer prayer. He may not drop a million dollars into your lap or supernaturally create a volume button on your child, but He does answer your requests. The key to this is praying that His will be done in your life. Part of using this key is the understanding of who God is as our Abba Father. One of Abba's desires is that none of us perish; He has given each of us opportunity to accept His gift.

His other desire is that we come to Him with all our needs, thoughts, prayers, and dreams. The other part is praying that His will be done. After reading Matthew 6:9-14, I realized that though my own father broke my heart, God wanted to restore it. Part of the restoration process and saying yes to my prayers included forgiving and praying unceasingly for my Dad.

God does answer prayer. God answered my heart's cry; my father is restored, redeemed, and living passionately for Christ. God broke the chains of addiction that enslaved my Dad all those years. We are now beginning the journey of establishing a relationship and building on the mutual foundation of our love for God. I'm so excited to be a "Daddy's girl" in more ways than one. My dad regrets all our childhood years he wasted, and each time he apologizes, I remind him I wouldn't have had it any other way. Our greatest blessings come from trials and pain. I gained freedom in forgiveness and communing with my heavenly Father while God worked on my Daddy's heart.

Life is about preparing for the future, discovering who we are and how God made us. There is one thing He wants us to know, one thing that will change us at our core: He longs to be our Abba Father. He longs to enter the door of your heart. He is waiting patiently; He is ready for you to cry out to Him with your hopes, your dreams, and your prayers. Pray unceasingly to God; come to Him with your innermost secrets and desires. He wants you to unleash His power and love. He is ready for you to take the lid off the box you put Him in. Are you ready to take that chance on Him?

Whether you barely know Him or you worship who He is, call out to Him. Ask Him to be your Father. This is one step I pray that God ignites in your mothering heart. Of all the names I've presented to you, this particular name and character of God is the stepping stone in knowing Him ever so intimately. He is ready for you to come to Him and, when you do, He will be like the father in the story of Luke. Instead of being dignified and sovereign, He's going to surprise the angels and all the hosts of heaven as He picks up his cloak and runs to your heart. His arms are ready to embrace you and celebrate your adoption as His child. In His name we can say AMEN!

Mama's Time-Out

- Has your earthly father caused you to see God in a different light? Write a letter to God. Ask Him to be your Father. Ask Him to change your heart.
- On the next two pages is "God's Love Letter" to you. Read it, let it take root deep in your heart, and share it with your friends and children.

Today's Love Note

My Child,

You may not know me, but I know everything about you.
Psalm 139:1

I know when you sit down and when you rise up.
Psalm 139:2

I am familiar with all your ways.
Psalm 139:3

Even the very hairs on your head are numbered.
Matthew 10:29-31

For you were made in my image.
Genesis 1:27

In me you live and move and have your being.
Acts 17:28

For you are my offspring.
Acts 17:28

I knew you even before you were conceived.
Jeremiah 1:4-5

I chose you when I planned creation.
Ephesians 1:11-12

You were not a mistake, for all your days are written in my book.
Psalm 139:15-16

I determined the exact time of your birth and where you would live.
Acts 17:26

You are fearfully and wonderfully made.
Psalm 139:14

I knit you together in your mother's womb.
Psalm 139:13

And brought you forth on the day you were born.
Psalm 71:6

I have been misrepresented by those who don't know me.
John 8:41-44

I am not distant and angry, but am the complete expression of love.
1 John 4:16

And it is my desire to lavish my love on you.
1 John 3:1

Simply because you are my child and I am your Father.
1 John 3:1

I offer you more than your earthly father ever could.
Matthew 7:11

For I am the perfect father.
Matthew 5:48

Every good gift that you receive comes from my hand.
James 1:17

For I am your provider and I meet all your needs.
Matthew 6:31-33

My plan for your future has always been filled with hope.
Jeremiah 29:11

Because I love you with an everlasting love.
Jeremiah 31:3

My thoughts toward you are countless as the sand on the seashore.
Psalm 139:17-18

And I rejoice over you with singing.
Zephaniah 3:17

I will never stop doing good to you.
Jeremiah 32:40

For you are my treasured possession.
Exodus 19:5

*I desire to establish you with
all my heart and all my soul.*
Jeremiah 32:41

*And I want to show you great
and marvelous things.*
Jeremiah 33:3

*If you seek me with all your heart,
you will find me.*
Deuteronomy 4:29

*Delight in me and I will give you
the desires of your heart.*
Psalm 37:4

For it is I who gave you those desires.
Philippians 2:13

*I am able to do more for you than
you could possibly imagine.*
Ephesians 3:20

For I am your greatest encourager.
2 Thessalonians 2:16-17

*I am also the Father who comforts
you in all your troubles.*
2 Corinthians 1:3-4

*When you are brokenhearted,
I am close to you.*
Psalm 34:18

*As a shepherd carries a lamb, I have
carried you close to my heart.*
Isaiah 40:11

*One day I will wipe away every
tear from your eyes.*
Revelation 21:3-4

*And I'll take away all the pain you have
suffered on this earth.*
Revelation 21:3-4

*I am your Father, and I love you even
as I love my son, Jesus.*
John 17:23

For in Jesus, my love for you is revealed.
John 17:26

*He is the exact representation
of my being.*
Hebrews 1:3

*He came to demonstrate that I am
for you, not against you.*
Romans 8:31

*And to tell you that I am not
counting your sins.*
2 Corinthians 5:18-19

*Jesus died so that you and I
could be reconciled.*
2 Corinthians 5:18-19

*His death was the ultimate expression
of my love for you.*
1 John 4:10

*I gave up everything I loved that
I might gain your love.*
Romans 8:31-32

*If you receive the gift of my son Jesus,
you receive me.*
1 John 2:23

*And nothing will ever separate you
from my love again.*
Romans 8:38-39

*Come home and I'll throw the biggest
party heaven has ever seen.*
Luke 15:7

*I have always been Father, and
will always be Father.*
Ephesians 3:14-15

My question is . . .Will you be my child?
John 1:12-13

I am waiting for you.
Luke 15:11-32

Love, Your Dad
Almighty God

Father's Love Letter used by permission of
Father Heart Communications
© 1999-2010 www.FathersLoveLetter.com

I Call Him By Name

Abba Father, Your love letter to me is spoken through Your Word. As I read it, I sense Your presence and thank You that You love me so much. I pray that You open my heart to boundaries unknown of Your love for me. Teach me what it means to be loved as Your child. Open my heart and my eyes to Your love as my Father. It fills my heart with awe and joy that You know the number of my days and the very hairs on my head. Lord, how amazing is the knowledge that You want to say yes to my prayers. Teach me to pray in Your will and open the floodgates of Your blessings as I journey into a deep relationship with You as my Abba. In Your Son's sweetest name I pray. AMEN!

Group Study and Discussion Guide

EL ROI—The God Who Sees Me

1. When do you feel your most invisible? Is it around your family, or around other women with strong careers? The Bible talks about how God is there and sees everything we do. In what ways does this strengthen your relationship with God?

2. Read Psalm 139:1-3. It tells us that God is familiar with all of our ways. He knows when we lie down and when we are on the move with our little ones. How does it speak to your heart?

3. Sometimes motherhood leaves us feeling unfulfilled because we aren't using our other talents. What talents do you possess besides being a mother? Of these talents, which ones can you develop or incorporate during your season of mothering?

YAHWEH JIREH—The Lord Will Provide

1. God wants us to look to Him for our every need. What worries do you have as a mother? Do you trust that God will provide all your needs?

2. Writing down God's provisions is just one of the many ways we can build our trust in Him. How have you kept a reminder of how God has provided?

EL CHAY—The Living God

1. In the chapters about learning our God is a living God, I shared my testimony of when I committed my life to Christ. If time allows and you feel comfortable, take turns sharing when you committed your life to God. Please note that what is said during this time is meant to be shared for your group's ears only. Share the significance of that choice. How has it changed you?

2. In your everyday walk as a mother and Christian, share how you stay connected with God. Is it through a Bible study? Do you set aside time for prayer every day?

3. I shared the story of the woman at the well in John 4. The verse we rested on was John 4:14. How do you identify with this woman?

4. As women, we battle so many issues, being thin, having the latest fashion, etc. I shared how God opened my eyes to my insecurities. What insecurities do you face? How do they affect your ability to see yourself as a child of God? How do they affect your ability to mother?

YAHWEH SHAMMAH—The Lord Is There

1. Yahweh Shammah is translated as "the Lord is there." It was originally a city that was named after God because people knew it was where God's presence resided. Take a moment to imagine what it would be like to not be able to close your eyes and talk to God as you do in prayer. How would this affect your relationship with God?

2. Losing a loved one is unspeakable. Losing a child scars your heart. As I shared stories about loss through my miscarriage, Dolly's loss of her sixteen-year-old son, and Amber's loss, what picture did this invoke about how the Lord was there to comfort us?

3. Have you had a loss? If you are comfortable sharing, would you share the ways God was there in the midst of your pain? Did He carry you through it?

MACHSEH—
God Is My Refuge

1. Our Father God was often referred to and called upon as a strong tower, a dwelling place, a place of refuge. Oftentimes in the days of old, King David referred to God as a place of refuge when the circumstances he was facing were too much to bear. How can you relate in the realms of motherhood?

2. I'm very transparent about sharing my depression after my son was born. The baby blues affect so very many moms. Have you been depressed? I believe in medication and walking with God to battle depression. What have you done to kick the baby blues?

3. When I need a time-out, I tell my kids, "Mommy is taking a time-out." I then retreat to my room, or the bathroom, lock the door so I can pray and gather my emotions and thoughts. How do you take refuge when you need it?

4. For one week, as a group, make it a challenge to memorize and meditate on Psalm 71:3. Then come back as a group and share how it affected your perspective, your thoughts, and your days!

ELOHIM—Creator

1. Rachel Scott's song, "I Wonder," is powerful. On your own time, either listen to her song on YouTube or purchase the CD. Then next time as a group, share what thoughts this song evoked.

2. Having children gives us a chance to see life through God's eyes. Not just life, but also how much He loves us. He loved us enough to send His only Son to die for us. What thoughts can you share about this mothering bond and how God loves you?

3. Children help renew our sense of awe in the world around us. How has having children changed your point of view?

EL SHADDAY—Almighty God

1. Take turns reading the story of Abram and Sarai in Genesis 17. Have you had difficulty getting pregnant and carrying a child to term? How do you relate to this story?

2. At one point in time, my desires for a new home, a Christian husband, and another child clouded out my desire to walk with God. I wanted these things more than I wanted to spend time with God. Read Psalm 37:4-5. Then take a sheet of paper and ask God to show each of you what desires He wants you to give up. You don't have to share this; however, pray together as a group that God will help each of you delight in Him.

3. On page 69, I shared a list of promises that God keeps. Which of these promises has God kept for you? Which of these promises do you need faith in God that He will keep?

EL OLAM—The Everlasting God

1. God is the only thing that is constant in our lives. Our children change through each stage from newborn, infancy, toddlerhood, preschooler... nothing ever stays the same, except God. How is this a comfort to you?

2. On a scale of 1 to 10, what is your need for consistency in your daily routine? What do you do to maintain consistency?

3. To maintain consistency, prepare your mindset to set limits and enforce them every time. What changes can you make to be consistent in your daily mothering routine?

YAHWEH ROI—
The Lord Is My Shepherd

1. The authors of the Bible use comparisons of work occupations in ancient times. One of the most prominent jobs to provide for family was to raise

sheep. Jesus often compared Himself to being a shepherd and His people to sheep. How does this word picture compare to our modern-day lives as mothers?

2. One of the most famous Scriptures of comfort is Psalm 23:1-3, "The Lord is my shepherd; I lack nothing. He makes me lie down in green pastures, he leads me beside quiet waters, he refreshes my soul. He guides me along the right paths for his name's sake." How does your life as a mother relate to this verse?

3. As a mother shepherding her young, how can you shepherd your children to obey your commands?

ESH OKLAH & EL KANNA—
God Is a Jealous God, God Is a Consuming Fire

1. God is referenced many times throughout the Bible as a jealous God and consuming fire. He is a God who is so concerned about our well-being that He becomes jealous when our attention is turned to other things. How can you achieve balance in serving God?

2. The day I stand before God, I pray that my job raising children to be passionate for Him was well done. How do you fan the flames to inspire your children to follow God?

3. Some of the lessons we can teach our children about God is through Bible stories, praying with them about hurts and concerns, and thanking Him for blessings. What areas do you lack and what ideas can you share with your group about igniting a passion for God?

4. In the chapter about American Idols, I challenged you with the Idol Evaluation. What were your results? Share your results with your group.

YAHWEH—Lord

1. We learned how holy and precious God's name is. In fact, when the Bible was written, some authors felt His name was too holy to write in full. Do you revere His name? If not, why?

2. To strengthen our resolve to proclaim we are followers of Christ, share a time when you were not ashamed to say you were a Christian. Now discuss an event when you were embarrassed or afraid to say that you were a Christian.

3. I shared how my daughter was in "bondage" to her bottle and how her iron will was severely affecting my sleep. Are your kids strong willed, or do they obey your commands? Review Hebrews 12:6-7.

4. As you parent your children, can you relate to God's discipline when He led the Israelites around the desert for forty years? In what areas do you still feel like you are leading your children through the desert to learn the same lesson? Read Deuteronomy 28:9-12 before you answer.

ADONAY—Master

1. There is a fine line between serving our families in love and being a doormat. As a mother, how do you teach your children to respect this boundary? What is the biggest challenge?

2. I was transparent about my dirty little secret of smoking and drinking. They became my masters because I turned to them instead of turning to God to cope with stress. Other times, I would use them to celebrate or for comfort. Because smoking and drinking are more extreme ideas of masters, I shared a list. Review the list and discuss which one was a master in your life: Selfishness, Laziness, Pride, Self-pity, Critical tongue, Judging others, Conceit, Comparisons, Bitterness, Self-exaltation, Materialism, Financial status, Emotional eating, Not placing Christ first.

3. How can you break the chains to this master? Review Psalm 135:14 and 2 Corinthians 5:17.

YAHWEH ROPHE—
The Lord Who Heals

1. Second Kings 20:5 is a powerful verse that reminds us God is our healer. Can you reflect in your life when God provided healing?
2. Watching our children go through illness causes our hearts to ache. I shared about a disease that debilitated my daughter's life and nearly caused long-term damage to Cheyenne's kidneys. We turned to God in prayer. When your child becomes sick, do you immediately ask God for protection and healing or do you call your doctor first? Why?
3. There is power when we come together and pray. Matthew 18:19-20: "Again, truly I tell you that if two of you on earth agree about anything they ask for, it will be done for them by my Father in heaven. For where two or three gather in my name, there am I with them." How does this scripture verse impact your quest in prayer?
4. Not all of us have a perfect walk as a Christ follower. Are you transparent with your mistakes in front of your children? If not, can you explain why?
5. Redemption is God's way of restoring our lives and bringing us into His family. Would you be willing to share your testimony of when you accepted Christ as your Savior? If not, write your story of redemption in your journal. Review what you've written and thank God for changing your life. If you need encouragement about God's redemption, visit my site: www.heather-riggleman.com.

YAHWEH SHALOM—
The Lord Is Peace

1. Sometimes we don't feel God's peace until we surrender what we are struggling with. What do you struggle with as a mom?
2. I love Marla's quote about her kids and sensing God's peace. She said, "Peace is knowing that God only loaned them [her kids] to me and they really aren't mine." What do you identify with in Marla's comment?
3. How do you experience God's peace in your life? How do you cultivate it in your heart and home?
4. I shared my experiences of my son's heart murmur and jaundice. Do you think God can use situations like mine to teach us to trust in Him? Why or why not?

YAHWEH NISSI—
The Lord Is My Banner

1. There is an unseen battle taking place in the spiritual realms; it is affecting our spiritual walks, especially because our children are discouraged to pray at school or say, "One nation under God." Have you encountered this in your personal relationship with God? How do you react?
2. Proverbs 22:6 reminds of how to train up our children. How are you training up your kids under God's banner?
3. Ephesians 6:18 is the basic Scripture for putting on the Lord's armor. Do you pray over your children? How can this be effective both in your everyday life and spiritual life?
4. Once we accept Jesus Christ in our hearts, we become adopted children of God. Our identities may have been compromised with feelings as an outsider or not feeling like we belong. How has this name of God opened your heart to His claim that you belong to Him?

ISH—Husband

1. I shared Tiffany's story of struggling as a single mom to be the provider and both parents to her child. Can you identify with her story? Have you ever thought of God as your husband who steps in the role of being a provider and father to your child? Why or why not?
2. Cassidy was transparent in her fears

about her son blaming God for their struggles and eventually walking away from Him. As a single mom or married mom, how can you set the example that God walks with us and has promised to be with us in times of trouble?

3. Being faithful has become more challenging in this day and age. What steps have you taken to protect your marriage? How does this affect your children?

4. God reminds us with His name as husband that He is captivated by us. He wants to protect and love us as a husband does. Have you ever thought of God in this way? What Scripture verses resonate this perspective?

SHOPPET—
The Lord Is My Judge

1. How we discipline our children is how they will view God. After I revealed the issues of discipline, what changes have you made in your parenting? Are you a compassionate judge?

2. As a group, look up and take turns reading James 4:12; John 8:15-16; John 12:47-49; 1 Peter 4:5, and 2 Timothy 4:1, 8. Then discuss the Scripture verses as they relate to parenting.

3. The chapter of "Frenemies" was by far the hardest to write. As a church body, we are to love one another, acting as Jesus' hands and feet. Have you been wounded by a Christian friend? Were you able to resolve it? Why or why not?

4. Look up Ephesians 4:29-32. Read the verses aloud. Ask God about relationships where you need to refrain from gossip and judgment. What does this reveal about your heart?

MIQWEH YISRAEL—
The Lord Is Hope

1. One of my favorite names of God is Miqweh Yisrael. He embodies the word hope. Can you share a story of when God has given you hope?

2. Read Psalm 71:4, and Psalm 130:5 & 7. Which Scripture do you identify with in your life in terms of hoping in God?

3. Take a notecard and write out Romans 5:1-5. Keep it in front of you throughout the week and read it as often as possible. Then reflect on the week and ask God to show how He has given you hope. Come back and share with your group.

4. I shared about my daughter's diagnosis of Asperger's and Inattentive ADD. Does your child have a disability? Did you feel hopeless? Have you taken your fears to God? Read all of Psalm 139 and apply it to your situation.

MELEK—The King of Kings

1. With all the earthquakes, starvation, violence, and bloodshed, it is difficult to keep the proper perspective that God is still the King of kings and has a plan. When you watch the evening news, do you find it difficult to believe that He is still in authority? Why or why not?

2. Read Romans 8:17. God didn't promise a perfect world; He did promise that we will share in His glory later on. How does this Scripture put the injustice of this world into proper perspective?

3. Review Romans 3:23, Ecclesiastes 7:20, 1 John 1:8, Romans 5:12, and 2 Peter 3:9. How do you respond to your child when she asks about something that has happened that was wrong? What do you tell her about God?

4. Because God is the King of kings, we are princesses in Christ. We are royalty. Have you thought of yourself as God's daughter? Why or why not?

5. Review the list on pages 186-187. If your self-esteem isn't full of God esteem, review this list. Tell yourself each day the statements listed. Ask God to heal your

heart and to help you believe this list as truth.

YAHWEH TSURI—
The Lord Is My Rock

1. Read 2 Samuel 22:3. How do you picture God as your rock?

2. Find a smooth stone and write the words, "The Lord is my rock" on it. Carry it with you to remind you of God's steadfastness.

3. Do you find it difficult to trust and rely on God in your life? What about as a mom?

4. Review Matthew 7:23-25. How much emphasis do you put on Jesus being the foundation of your home? Share examples with your group.

ABBA—Father, Daddy

1. This is by far my favorite name of God. He is mighty and commands respect in the throne room, but behind closed doors, He is our Father. Did you have a good or poor example of an earthly father?

2. Have you been the prodigal child like the story in Luke 15? If so, what brought you back to your Father God?

3. Review Psalm 27:10. How does it make you feel to know God receives you as His child?

4. Review The Father's Love Letter. Which Scripture verses in this letter stand out to you?

A Few Thoughts

Everyone thinks it's so easy to sit down and write a book. It's not. There are grammar, technical rules, and of course, learning software programs. Not to mention research and finding the time to put it all into words that others will love and want to read. Writing this book wouldn't have been possible without the immense patience and encouragement of a few people.

Chris, my husband, I haven't found a man who could have been as patient as you. Thank you for sacrificing time, energy, and your sanity with the kids so I could write on the weekends. All those nights of pizza, mac & cheese, and running out of towels was worth it.

Marlene Bangull, my editor. Without reigning me in and showing me the how to's of writing, this would still be in my head and not on paper. Thank you!

Mary Keely, you have an eye for a treasure hidden in the weeds. Thank you for looking past the raw material and taking a chance.

Angela Loven, my best friend and sister in Christ. Had you not led me to Jesus, none of this would have ever happened. Thank you for leaving all those "Are you mad at me?" messages. Love you.

Audra Waugh, my other best friend. When I flop, you flip, we're flip-flop friends. You helped me formalize my thoughts into a story and kept me grounded when I wanted to run. Love you much.

Aliisa, Terri, Tamara, Pauline, and Robbi: Thank you for being there when I was ready to quit, for reading the rough drafts, and for celebrating every little milestone!

Anonymous and Sonrise Mamas. Y'all helped in the form of prayers and finances. Without you, this journey to write never would have started. Thank you for helping with editing in the form of a $1200.00 check and for sending me to my first writer's conference. And to Jean Heuser for believing in me.

Daddy, the angels are still celebrating at your adoption into Christ's family. Thank you for intercessory prayers and walking with me in my struggles. Love you.

Mom, if I hear one more, "I told you so," I may scream. Yes, I should have majored in English like you told me.

Recommended Resources:

- "Resolution," album by Rachel Scott
- Christian music for your kids that won't drive you bonkers: www.gofishguys.com
- *Heaven Is For Real* by Todd Burpo
- *Heaven Has Blue Carpet: A Sheep Story by a Suburban Housewife* by Sharon Niedzinski
- *Scouting The Divine: My Search For God in Wine, Wool, and Wild Honey* by Margaret Feinberg
- *God's Little Princess Devotional Bible Story Book* by Sheila Walsh
- *Raising Up Girls* by Dr. James Dobson
- *Bringing Up Boys* by Dr. James Dobson
- *Creative Correction: Extraordinary Ideas for Everyday Discipline* by Lisa Whelchel

Informational Websites:

- Mothers of Preschoolers: www.mops.org
- Women of Faith: www.wof.org
- Moms in Touch: www.momsintouch.org
- Autism or Asperger's: www.autismspeaks.org
- Inattentive ADD or ADHD: www.4-adhd.org

Sources:

CHAPTER 5
Russell Kelfer. *You Are Who You Are For a Reason*. © 2001 *Praise For The Planner, Praise For The Plan*. Used by permission. Discipleship Tape Ministries, Inc. 10602 Mossbank San Antonio, Texas 78230.

CHAPTER 6
Beth Moore, *So Long, Insecurity* (Carol Stream, IL: Tyndale House Publishers, 2010, xiii). Quote from Larry Richards, *Every Name of God in the Bible* (Nashville: Thomas Nelson Publishing, 2001), 44.

CHAPTER 8
Lois Tiffany. *So Be It: Let Not Your Heart Be Troubled*. New Hope Books, 1992. Taken from the blog http://christianartsongs.blogspot.com/2009/04/sobeit.html. Used by permission.

CHAPTER 9
Larry Richards, *Every Name of God in the Bible* (Nashville: Thomas Nelson, 2001), 79.

CHAPTER 10
All names of God are referenced from Larry Richards, *Encyclopedia of Bible Words* (Grand Rapids: Zondervan, 2001).

CHAPTER 11
Referenced from Larry Richards, *Every Name of God in the Bible* (Nashville: Thomas Nelson, 2001).

CHAPTER 12
Bruce Wilkinson and David Kopp, *The Dream Giver* (Colorado Springs: Multnomah Books, 2003). Rachel Scott, *I Wonder*. Indelible Creative Group/Word. © 2008 Composition. Used by permission.

CHAPTER 17
Sharon Niedzinskil, *Heaven Has Blue Carpet* (Nashville: Thomas Nelson, 2008). Larry Richards, *Every Name of God in the Bible* (Nashville: Thomas Nelson, 2001), 85-87.

CHAPTER 21
Larry Richards, *Encyclopedia of Bible Words* (Grand Rapids: Zondervan, 2001).

CHAPTER 23
Larry Richards, *Every Name of God in the Bible* (Nashville: Thomas Nelson, 2001).

CHAPTER 25
Larry Richards, *Every Name of God in the Bible* (Nashville: Thomas Nelson, 2001).

CHAPTER 27
All quotes taken from friends, used with permission.

CHAPTER 31
Jennifer Wolf, *About.com*. http://singleparents.about.com/od/legalissues/p/portrait.htm (accessed Oct 10, 2010).

CHAPTER 33
Larry Richards, *Encyclopedia of Bible Words* (Grand Rapids: Zondervan, 2001), 363–368.

CHAPTER 35
Larry Richards, *Encyclopedia of Bible Words* (Grand Rapids: Zondervan, 2001), 343–345.

CHAPTER 39
Larry Richards, *Encyclopedia of Bible Words* (Grand Rapids: Zondervan, 2001), 537–538.

CHAPTER 42
Father's Love Letter. Father Heart Communications © 1999–2010 www.FathersLoveLetter.com. Accessed, February 13, 2012. Used by permission.

CPSIA information can be obtained at www.ICGtesting.com
Printed in the USA
LVOW082248040512

280375LV00001B/28/P